— ROSES —
from Dreams
to Reality

— ROSES —
from Dreams
to Reality

STUMP PUBLISHING COMPANY
121 NORTH SULTANA AVENUE
ONTARIO, CALIFORNIA 91764

Swim, Herb
Roses - from Dreams to Reality

ISBN 0-937594-14-8

Printed in the United States of America

TABLE
OF
CONTENTS

A.R.B.A NEWSLETTER   June 1992

Editorial Comment

The 1992 Annual was despatched to all paid up members in April; subsequent new members should also have received their copy. If any member has not received their 1992 Annual, please let the editors know, as there are still some copies available.

Needless to say the production of the Annual was not without it's trials and tribulations, however we are reasonably happy with the outcome, but at considerable cost to the association. The annual has been well received, and the editors would like to take this opportunity to thank all contributors for all the material published.

If our publications are going to be lively, interesting and topical, we need the material to print. So do let us have your articles, letters, views, hints and tips, anything which you think may be of interest for our 1993 Annual.

Hope to meet many of you at the A.R.B.A. Stand at Hampton Court.

Best Wishes

John and Margaret

GOING FOR GOLD

At the Hampton Court International Flower Show in July, ARBA will be staging a competitive exhibit. Members who can assist in any way from Tuesday 7th July to Sunday 12th July inclusive, please contact Bernhard Mehring, telephone 0734 695658. All members who will be exhibiting their seedlings and require exhibitors' passes, contact Bernhard Mehring for registration.

ANNUAL GENERAL MEETING
Of
THE AMATEUR ROSE BREEDERS ASSOCIATION

Members are invited to attend the ARBA Annual General Meeting at 1.30 p.m. at The Gardens Of The Rose, St. Albans, on Saturday, 12th September, 1992. Most members meet earlier in the Trial Grounds to view and discuss members' seedlings.

AGENDA

1.   Apologies
2.   Chairmans's Address
3.   Minutes of the 1991 A.G.M.
4.   Reports –

   a) Secretary
   b) Treasurer
   c) ARBA Test Garden Registration
   d) Editors
   e) ARBA Test Garden
   f) Lauriston Sponsorship Scheme
   g) Heaton Park

5.   Election of Officers
6.   Rose Breeding Convention
7.   Rose Naming/Registration/Fees
8.   Heaton Park – ARBA Test Garden
9.   Membership Subscriptions
10.   Venues for 1993
11.   Any other business

Members wishing to have any other items included on the agenda, which cannot be dealt with under (11) should notify the Secretary in writing before 1.8.1992.

LAURISTON SPONSORSHIP SCHEME

Contributors to the scheme will be aware of the ups and downs with the scheme, It is, however, still going strong, and new entries of members' seedlings are requested for this autumn. It will be of considerable assistance in marketing members' seedlings if seedlings are entered before September. Anyone new to the scheme should contact Bernhard Mehring please for details.

SYMPOSIUM ON AFTERCARE OF SEEDLINGS

Members' contributions are urgently sought on this very interesting topic. Most members have had problems (downy mildew, damping off, transplant problems, etc.) with aftercare of their seedlings and will, judging by recent successes have found solutions to such problems.

Derrick Everitt has agreed to compile the information for the next annual and contributions should be sent to him. Address: Mr Derrick Everitt, 48 Shrewsbury Fields, Shifnal, Shropshire, TF11 8AN

HAMPTON COURT: STOP PRESS

Due to last minute changes all exhibits must be staged by 1830 hrs 7th July prior to judging at 1900 hrs. Will all members who can supply blooms and give any assistance in staging, please arrange to be at Hampton Court by midday on the above date. Members please note that in effect we will be staging three shows, and will require blooms for Tuesday/Wednesday, Thursday/Friday, and Saturday/Sunday. Any queries please contact Bernhard Mehring 0734 695658 or Bill Bossom 081 363 7210.

NAMING AND REGISTRATION OF SEEDLINGS

Concern has been expressed that amateur rose breeders may be registering too many seedlings and that they may be exploited. It has therefore been thought advisable to place this subject on the agenda for the A.G.M. for discussion. Members, who have been contacted by members of the public, as a result of the list of breeders distributed by ARBA , to make a rose available for naming, (other than the Lauriston Sponsorship Scheme) should advise Derrick Everitt as soon as possible with details, i.e. roses made available, fee, name and has it been registered. This will allow Management Committee to assess the situation and then advise members to their own advantage.

NATIONAL ROSE QUIZ

The National Rose Quiz was this year hosted by the Rhondda Rose Society, and was held at the Parc & Dare Hall at Treorchy on the 10th May.

The questions were set by Peter Harkness, who was also the Question Master. Six teams took part in a very closely fought contest. The eventual winners were the team representing Lincoln Rose Society; two members of the team were also ARBA members

Next year the quiz is being hosted by the West Midlands Rose Society in late April. Now is the time to think about ARBA forming a team to try and repeat the magnificent win of 1988.

Any members wishing to participate, please contact the editors.

ACKNOWLEDGEMENTS

Occasionally a rose friend has suggested that I write a book on rose breeding. This was flattering but did not inspire any action. It was not immediately apparent what form such a book must take to be made readable and useful. It was readily apparent that it would be necessary to set aside time from a schedule already as full as I needed to feel satisfactorily occupied so the decision became a matter involving priorities.

About two years ago my good friend and mentor, Dr. Walter E. Lammerts, suggested that I should take on this job on behalf of the increasing number of amateur rose breeders. I agreed to do this in the form of an autobiography of a rose breeder if he would proof read my manuscript and be free with suggestions as to how it might be improved. He agreed and has read the rough and corrected draft making most helpful suggestions. At one point he wrote some information on the "how to" of rose breeding which I have asked his permission to include at the end of this book. His support has kept me at the job.

More recently my friend and neighbor, John D. "Jack" O'Neil, of Upland, a Consulting Rosarian of The American Rose Society, has read a later draft and made a number of helpful suggestions that have been adopted.

My wife, Helen, has patiently read every word of every draft and has kept me from misspelling some. She has been a continuing source of encouragement and helpful suggestions. She has also been available to respond to ideas from me - both positively and negatively.   This would not have gotten off the ground without her support.

My elder daughter, Sarajane Swim Wallace, is primarily an educator but she also has an artistic talent which she has used to help me explain the parts of a rose flower useful to a rose breeder in the one diagram in this book.

I am most grateful to each for their unique contribution and to each goes my sincere thanks.

H.C.S.

FOREWORD

Why does one write a book? Why did I write this book? I have not thought about the answer to such questions until the second question was posed to me.

My own interest in roses and rose breeding has been a lifelong experience. It has been deeply fascinating for me and I am convinced that all rose breeders find it so whether it be for them a vocation or an avocation. The more serious one's involvement in this occupation, the more important is a grasp of the history of roses. So I look on this book as primarily history. It involves the activities of other breeders as well as my own. The contribution of other American rose breeders has so far gone largely untold except for the various editions of Modern Roses and scattered writings in The American Rose Magazine and American Rose Annual. When their product is used by other breeders it becomes a key to rose history. Many foreign breeders have made important achievements in this sense, and this is dealt with in the pages of this book.

So, the book is offered especially to amateur breeders with the hope that it may contain not only information, but ideas that they can use productively. I have included some of the reasoning that went into my crosses, especially the more important ones. My failures have not all gone unrecorded either, as one does learn from mistakes. As Tom Wilson in a Universal Press Syndicate cartoon has it: "Remember Ziggy . . . Good judgement comes from experience . . . and experience comes from poor judgement!!"

Beyond this, it is hoped that readers will find the book entertaining. The bit about genetics in the early part may be heavy for some, but it is included because it can be helpful. It is not essential as many successful plant breeders knew nothing about the subject.

Lastly, some ego indulgence has been involved in the production of this treatise. One does not relish the thought of a life's work being lost in the mists of time.

SUTTER'S GOLD AARS-1950
(CHARLOTTE ARMSTRONG X SIGNORA)

SHOW GIRL =
JOANNA HILL X CRIMSON GLORY

AUSTRIAN COPPER = ROSA FOETIDA BICOLOR
A significant ancestor.

ANGEL FACE - AARS-1969
[(CIRCUS X LAVENDER PINOCCHIO) X STERLING SILVER]

DOUBLE DELIGHT - AARS-1977
(GRANADA X GARDEN PARTY)

OKLAHOMA = CHRYSLER IMPERIAL X
CHARLES MALLERIN

Above: **FANDANGO** = CHARLOTTE ARMSTRONG X
(PRESIDENT HERBERT HOOVER X MRS. SAM MCGREDY)

Below: **SIGNORA** = JULIEN POTIN X
SENSATION.   A significant parent.

ROYAL HIGHNESS - AARS-1963
(VIRGO X PEACE)

CHARLOTTE ARMSTRONG
AARS-1941
[SOEUR (SISTER) THERESE X CRIMSON GLORY]
A very important parent.

Below:
CHRYSLER IMPERIAL
(CHARLOTTE ARMSTRONG X MIRANDY)

Above: **GARDEN PARTY** - AARS-1960
(CHARLOTTE ARMSTRONG X PEACE)

JUNO =
DUQUESA DE
PENARANDA
X CHARLOTTE
ARMSTRONG

Above: **HELEN TRAUBEL** AARS-1952
(CHARLOTTE ARMSTRONG X GLOWING SUNSET)

Below: **CRIMSON GLORY** = CATHRINE KORDES
SEEDLING X W. E. CHAPLIN.
An important ancestor of red roses.

BUCCANEER = GOLDEN RAPTURE
X (MAX KRAUSE X CAPT. THOMAS

PINK PARFAIT - AARS-1961
(FIRST LOVE X PINOCCHIO)

FORTY-NINER -
AARS-1949
(CONTRAST X
CHARLOTTE
ARMSTRONG)

Left: **CIRCUS** - AARS-1956
(FANDANGO X PINOCCHIO)

FIRST LOVE =
CHARLOTTE ARMSTRONG
X SHOW GIRL

FLORADORA - AARS-1945
(BABY CHATEAU X ROSA ROXBURGHI)
A very important parent.

MISTER LINCOLN AARS-1965
(CHRYSLER IMPERIAL X CHARLES MALLERIN)

MOJAVE - AARS-1954
(CHARLOTTE ARMSTRONG X SIGNORA)

MONTEZUMA = FANDANGO X FLORADORA

Chapter 1

THE BEGINNING

The first roses in my memory were in the front yard of my parents home on a farm in North Central Oklahoma. The only ones I can clearly remember are the red and the yellow ones. These were not the only colors there. The pinks just did not impress me. Clearly recalled is at least one very dark red one that must have been a member of the Hybrid Perpetual Class - popular in the early 1900's. There was only one yellow rose in that garden and it was a shrub just outside my bedroom window. During the flowering season I would look outside each morning to see if any new flowers had appeared on that yellow during the night. The variety's name is not known but it probably was HARISON'S YELLOW -widely planted in that time. It was the custom to obtain "slips" from friends, neighbors and/or relatives. Every housewife knew how to root them.

After seventy-five years about all that is remembered of the two roses are their colors. The red was very dark red, very double and quite irregular in form while the yellow was bright and the petals loosely arranged. Since no yellow rose of that time was "bright" yellow the partial shade that it received probably accounted for the brightness of color. Then it could have been just the romance in my eyes as that was the beginning of a love affair with the rose! In retrospect it is obvious that yellow and dark red roses were a dominant lifelong interest and that more effort was devoted to improving roses in these colors than in any others.

1

My early interest in horticulture was not confined just to roses. My parents had about five acres devoted to various kinds of fruit - mostly apples but with a pear or two, two pie cherry trees and several varieties of American grapes (Vitis labruscana). The names of the grapes especially liked still come to mind -CONCORD, NIAGARA and DELAWARE. Father had planted only one or two peach varieties in that original orchard and they were dying of old age in my time.

As a small boy on the farm my entertainment was somewhat limited as to variety. I liked to read so all books and newspapers were devoured from cover to cover. Somewhere an advertisement by Stark Brother's Nursery and Orchard Company came to my attention. It described some apple and peach varieties in such glowing terms that Mother was asked to send for the free catalogue offered. When it came it was apparent to me that our orchard could no longer do without some of the ones so beautifully pictured. My parents apparently did not want to dampen my enthusiasm so ordered one tree each of about four apple varieties and perhaps a half dozen peach varieties. One peach named "CHAMPION" proved to be a grand success but the rest were not. The father of my closest friend, whom I visited occasionally, was a neighbor who had a twenty acre apple orchard with some excellent varieties in it - an increasingly attractive place to go.

Our family moved to town when I was thirteen and little was seen of either roses or apples for a good many years. High school and college followed. It seemed clear from an early age that a livelihood in some form of agriculture would be pleasant — my ignorance of how that might be done was boundless. Somewhat blindly I enrolled in the School of Agriculture at what was then Oklahoma A and M College (now Oklahoma State University). I found chemistry tedious but a course in Plant Genetics was fascinating. It was taught by a Professor Griffee who caught my attention the first day of class by discussing the inheritance of eye color in humans. He described genetics as the "mathematics of chance." I had always enjoyed math and soon found the new form exciting. My grade of A+ was the only one in the class. I had learned belatedly the secret to good grades was to get interested in the subject. It was not clear how one could make a living in this field at that time other than to teach it and teaching did not appeal to me. Later an opportunity was presented me to pursue a doctorate in Plant Genetics (necessary to teaching it at the college or university level) but it was not grasped because teaching still did not appeal to me.

In the meantime it had become necessary to choose a major course of study. I decided it would be "Pomology" (the Study and Culture of Pome Fruits) in the Department of Horticulture and Forestry. It was learned that "pome fruits" included not only apples, pears and the stone fruits but strawberries and blackberries among others. I did not know at that time this family included roses nor that the family name was "ROSACEAE."

By the time college graduation arrived job opportunities looked bleak. Landscape Architecture sounded glamorous so a post-graduate year was spent at Iowa State College (Iowa State University now). At the end of that time in 1928 the best prospect for a job seemed to be as a trainee under a golf course architect. The job took me to Santa Catalina Island off the coast of Southern California. It was October and cold and damp - the slow time of year - and no way to get home. My closest family was an aunt and uncle in Pasadena. After three months I quit and applied for a job near Glendale at another golf course. This lasted for about six months but when a job opportunity at Coolidge Rare Plant Gardens became available in Pasadena it was grasped eagerly. To my dismay it was discovered at the end of the first week that the pay was eighteen dollars a week. I had not asked about that detail when applying for the job. The foreman gave out the information that new employees were all started at eighteen dollars per week and at the end of the first month were either given a raise of two dollars a week or let go. This was discouraging but being an optimist it was not defeating. I fully expected that I would get a raise - and I did. Work at Coolidge Gardens began just six weeks before "Black Tuesday" on Wall Street in October 1929.

Amid the hardships of the times some good things happened. Coolidge Gardens had a side specialty of growing standard ("tree") roses. Dwight Coolidge, a world famous plantsman and importer -introducer of exotic plants, several years before my arrival, had discovered a chance rose seedling. He propagated it and used it as a standard (tree rose) rootstock and budded garden rose varieties on it. He named it IXL. With a smooth dark green stem it was superior in appearance to all other rootstocks being used for standards at that time. The tree roses produced by Coolidge found an eager market both at retail and at wholesale. I.X.L. is listed in Modern Roses 6 as resulting from a cross of TAUSEND-

3

SCHON X VIELCHENBLAU. If we can put credence in the "common knowledge" that prevailed at Coolidge Gardens we would believe that Mr. Coolidge found the rose seedling in the immediate vicinity of these two roses named as its parents. Under the circumstances it is obvious that the seedling was not produced as a controlled cross. I have always thought that Mr. Coolidge was a skilled enough plantsman that his "guess"as to the origin of I.X.L. coupled with the fact that the seedling carried prominently characters of both projected parents gave the presumed cross enough validy to satisfy me. Let's face it, the parentage of many of the early rose hybrids were not known as a result of controlled crosses but were intelligent guesses. I am willing to rely on many of them because of the proven skill of their originator-introducers.

From my first day assigned duties involved various activities related to roses - mostly tree roses but some bush and climbing ones as well. One of the jobs was to cut off the tops of recently budded tree roses in order to make them branch. This pruning back occurred just at the peak of bloom. The blooms just fell on the ground - a terrible waste in my eyes. GOLDEN EMBLEM was a relatively new rose at that time and Coolidge Gardens grew quite a lot of it on trees. The rich yellow of that McGredy rose with the bright red blush on the outer petals did much to fix the name of Sam McGredy in my memory. (This was the grandfather of the present Samuel McGredy IV.)

While enduring layoffs and unemployment in the early half of 1930 an advancement to rose foreman was offered and accepted. Unfortunately three years went by without a pay increase so a job was applied for at Armstrong Nurseries in Ontario, California. I went to work there in January 1934. The new job required divided attention - sales clerk during the winter and foreman-trainee in the rose department the rest of the year. Where Coolidge Gardens grew a few thousand rose plants, Armstrong Nurseries grew hundreds of thousands and had customers, both wholesale and retail, all over the world.

In the meantime President Hoover had signed into law in May 1930 an extension to the Patent Act to cover plants. The protection would be known as a Plant Patent. Soon some large nursery firms applied for protection for some roses on which they had exclusive distribution rights in the United States. This inspired the installing of a Research Department at Armstrong Nurseries in July 1935 and Dr. Walter E. Lammerts was hired to set

4

it up.   Trained at the University of California he was already known as a successful breeder of snapdragons but had no experience with and little knowledge of rose varieties.   Various individuals at Armstrong assisted him in this respect.   It was my pleasure and opportunity to be of assistance.   Dr. Lammerts was assigned breeding projects in not only roses but stone fruits (peaches, nectarines and apricots) and the bramble berries as well.   An interesting objective connected to the fruit breeding was aimed at producing new peach and nectarine varieties with shorter "winter chilling requirement" than existing varieties in order that they might be grown and sold with satisfaction in California and particularly in Southern California. Prior to the onset of the breeding program at Armstrongs several winters had followed one another in which there had been relatively high temperatures, light rainfall and much aborting of flowers in the commercial peach orchards of Southern California.   This also resulted in what was then called "delayed foliation" (later "prolonged dormancy") in peach orchards and attendant crop failures.

Chapter 2

PLANT RESEARCH AT ARMSTRONG NURSERIES

Dr. Lammerts' experience with roses, prior to his employment as Director of Research at Armstrong Nurseries, was limited pretty much to catalogue pictures and what he was told by fellow employees.   Basic genetic knowledge led him to immediately set up experiments to gain insight into inheritance.   One instance of this was his harvesting a quantity of seed from the cultivar named DAINTY BESS - a single pink, quite popular in that day.   He reasonably assumed that a large part of the seed would have resulted from self pollination.   When all the seedlings had flowers with just five petals he concluded that singleness was a "recessive" trait and that any pure single (ie. only five petals) crossed with any other pure single would result in all five-petaled offspring.

This is the kind of research that Gregor Mendel would have approved.   I do not want to make this a technical treatise on rose breeding because in my opinion a knowledge of Mendel's Law is not an essential to successful and/or fun rose breeding.   Horticulture history is full of the achievements of plant breeders with no formal training in genetics who made great contributions in breeding new cultivars.   Albert Einstein is quoted as saying: "Imagination is more important than knowledge," and I think this applies to rose breeding.   The science of genetics has made remarkable strides in the last two or three decades after almost a century of quiet.   Even though it is believed that a knowledge of plant genetics is not essential (and this applies particularly to my subject) perhaps a simple explanation of Mendelian "Theory" will be helpful.   Some

7

wild roses (species) are relatively simple in their genetic makeup but some are not and nearly all garden roses of today have a more or less complex genetic structure. The simpler forms are called "diploid," meaning that all parts of the plant except the sexual parts have two sets of seven chromosomes in each cell. The chromosomes have been pictured as like sausage links. Within these links are still smaller parts of the cell called genes which carry within their tiny protein bodies one to many "orders" that "tell" the plant what it is to become during its life span. (The explanation for this has become much more sophisticated today but the foregoing will suffice for my purpose.) Most garden roses of today have a more complex genetic makeup. A great majority of them have four sets of seven chromosomes referred to as "tetraploid" (twenty eight in all) making the problem of exploring for inheritance traits far more complicated. Collecting the wild (simple) roses that went into todays garden roses and growing self-pollinated seedlings from them has seemed impractical for both the hobbyist and the commercial breeder. Rose breeding then begins to take on more the aspects of an art than a science.

Dr. Lammerts in his first year made self pollinations and experimental crosses, germinated and grew the resulting seed. As the seedlings grew large enough he indexed each population (family of seedlings) and reached some preliminary decisions about the inheritance of a number of character-traits. The growing of seedlings of DAINTY BESS mentioned earlier exemplify this. Perhaps putting this in a simple chart form for one trait will best illustrate the procedure.

Let D = a gene for double (more than five petals).

Let d = a gene for single (five petals).

In the simplest form of rose, in the wild for instance, the genetic complement for petalage could be illustrated as follows:

DD = two genes for doubleness = a many petaled flower.

Dd = one gene for doubleness and one for singleness = a double (possibly indistinguishable from DD above but usually with some diminishing of petal count).

dD = similar to Dd above.

dd = a single or five petaled rose.

Dr. Lammerts knew the number of chromosomes represented in the sex cells, ie. pollen (male) and ovule (female), would be only

8

half that in the cells of the rest of the plant and that they would be randomly sorted at the time of pollination, combining to be represented in a new individual cultivar-hybrid cultivated variety. (I will use "variety" here). Its genetic makeup for petalage in that event could be represented as dddd. When self-polinated nothing but dddd (single) roses could result. This is called "pure strain recessive." If DAINTY BESS chromosomes contained even one of the "dominant" D genes the flower would have had more than five petals. The distribution of the genes controlling petal count in seedlings may be represented in the following chart of a tetraploid rose with one dominant D gene and three recessive d genes selfed (Dddd $). Let us represent the gametes (sex genes) for each sexual parent as follows:

Female (seed parent) = Dd + Dd + Dd + dd + dd + dd

Male (pollen parent) = Dd + Dd + Dd + dd + dd + dd

It is possible for these gametes to combine at pollination into the combinations shown in Figure 1 below. Since the combinations are at random (chance) it would be necessary to produce a very large population of seedlings from the cross to get the results in the precise proportions as illustrated:

Fig. 1. The combinations are called "zygotes." They represent the genes for petalage:

DDdd + DDdd + DDdd + Dddd + Dddd + Dddd +

DDdd + DDdd + DDdd + Dddd + Dddd + Dddd +

DDdd + DDdd + DDdd + Dddd + Dddd + Dddd +

Dddd + Dddd + Dddd + dddd + dddd + dddd +

Dddd + Dddd + Dddd + dddd + dddd + dddd +

Dddd + Dddd + Dddd + dddd + dddd + dddd +

Only the dddd zygotes would be single flowered (ie. five petals). In theory perhaps it should be possible to distinguish the DDdd forms from the Dddd ones but it may not be. The point to this is that the "D" gene is the dominant one and the "d" is the recessive one and when they are in the same zygote only the dominant one will be expressed.

In a tetraploid rose we do know there are normally twenty eight chromosomes. We do not know how many genes there are. We believe each gene carries a directive for each character but may account for more than one character. Together they

9

account for every part of a plant.   To illustrate this let me mention some of the parts of a rose which must get its appearance from one or more genes.   I have dealt with petal count but there is also petal length, width, shape (with variations), color (with variations), etc.   One or more genes determine leaf shape, color, size, conformation, thickness, surface texture; the same with regard to the pattern of prickles (thorns), their shape, size, number, pattern, etc.   This goes on and on for every last part of the rose as it does for every living plant (or animal).   In the case of red color for a rose Marshall and Collicut* stated in 1983 that three groups of anthocyanins may contribute to red color in roses and that each group may be represented by two or more forms.   I did not know all this in the 1940s but in observing various named varieties and seedlings from them an intuitive feeling about the interrelationship of pigments and the quantitative significance of certain pigments developed.   This was fortified by making various experimental crosses in an attempt to get answers to "what if" questions - what would happen if such and such a cross were made.   It is of interest that our intuitive conclusions so closely approach the scientific ones reached thirty years later.

Eugene Boerner made a cross of PINOCCHIO X CRIMSON GLORY that gave him FASHION, a 1950 AARS Award and what was called a "color break."   I did not know of his success until I had already secured what could have been called FASHION'S "baby half-sister."   A cross of WORLD'S FAIR X PINOCCHIO resulted in a Floribunda somewhat more compact in habit than FASHION but with the same "color break."   Although Modern Roses 8 describes ANGELIQUE (my rose) as "coral pink to salmon pink" and FASHION as "coral-peach" a close comparison of the flowers would find them nearly indistinguishable in color.   Since both CRIMSON GLORY and WORLD'S FAIR were the output of Wilhelm Kordes of Germany my curiosity was aroused - what did they have in common in their ancestry?   I was not particularly surprised to learn that WORLD'S FAIR was a seedling resulting from the cross of DANCE OF JOY X CRIMSON GLORY.   The published parentage of CRIMSON GLORY told me little as one was a seedling (not described) and the other was W.E. CHAPLIN, a variety whose parentage was not published.   I did find it of interest

*NOTE: H. H. Marshall and L.M. Collicut: "Breeding For Red Colors In Roses" - 1983 American Rose Annual.

to learn that DANCE OF JOY was a derivative of PAUL's SCARLET CLIMBER because I knew that variety as a red with a minimum of blue as it aged - the same character I found notable in WORLD'S FAIR. The red of WORLD'S FAIR was a deeper tone suggesting an accumulation of the desirable trait I was searching for.

Dr. Lammerts agreed early to conduct a seminar on several subjects dealing with plants. The one that interested me the most was the one on genetics. This provided an opportunity to brush up on a subject that had been most fascinating in college. Dr. Lammerts was a fine moderator, enhancing the interest of his students. He asked me to help in indexing the traits of his rose seedlings - an interesting chore. It is recalled that one character he was evaluating was glossiness of leaf. This was a variable that necessitated some degree of arbitrariness in determining where to classify each individual seedling. I did the best I could. Walter (I had come to call him that by this time) concluded that glossy leaf was dominant to non-glossy or dull. This was a trait that was a bit elusive. It could have been a case where dominance was not complete as is sometimes the case. It was my position that glossy leaves were preferable to dull and no one seemed to disagree. It was soon concluded that yellow and white flower color were recessive to red but that red flower color would be diluted by genes for yellow or white - another case of incomplete dominance. The red crossed to yellow and/or white resulted in pink in varying degree depending on the number of genes for red color available in the red parent and the chance distribution to the offspring.

Two red roses quite popular in the 1920s and early 1930s were HADLEY and HOOSIER BEAUTY, introduced in 1914 and 1915 respectively. HADLEY was a very fragrant rose but had a strong purplish tint and this became dominant as the flower opened. It also was extremely susceptible to mildew. HOOSIER BEAUTY had a much purer red color and while the foliage was sparse it resisted mildew much better than HADLEY. An inevitable comparison of the two popular varieties of the day led one to a conviction that for color at least HOOSIER BEAUTY was the more desirable. When ETOILE DE HOLLANDE was introduced in 1919 it easily eclipsed both the older two in color. In the terminology of the day both HADLEY AND HOOSIER BEAUTY were described as "Crimson" - HADLEY as "rich crimson" and HOOSIER BEAUTY as "glowing crimson shading darker."

ETOILE DE HOLLANDE on the other hand was described as "bright red - a standard for comparison among red roses." It is of interest to look at the published parentage of these three old roses:

HADLEY = (LIBERTY X RICHMOND) X GENERAL MACARTHUR

HOOSIER BEAUTY = RICHMOND X CHATEAU DE CLOS VOGET

ETOILE DE HOLLANDE = GENERAL MACARTHUR X HADLEY

If RICHMOND were ever observed I do not remember it. GENERAL MACARTHUR and LIBERTY are well remembered as purplish reds. It seems incredible that ETOILE DE HOLLANDE could have resulted from a cross of GENERAL MACARTHUR X HADLEY as it had so little of the purple. Justified fully, for "Etoile's" introduction time, was the phrase in MODERN ROSES "a standard for comparison among red roses." On the other hand the variety CHATEAU DE CLOS VOGET from Pernet-Ducher was a mystery rose with no published parentage. It is recalled that from an early date I believed the freedom from bluing in red roses was possibly due to the influence of genes for yellow pigment. In any event there was an awareness of the importance of searching for breeding material among existing red roses that might put the blue "away" to such a degree that it did not show up in a red rose even as it aged. When Dr. Lammerts started the breeding program at Armstrong Nurseries the best reds available included CRIMSON GLORY, NIGHT AND ETOILE DE HOLLANDE. Preliminary crosses showed the latter contributed little to the red rose family and perhaps a look at its parentage should have been a tipoff to the probable traits of its offspring. Its inability to pass on improved red color, its short buds and its lack of mildew resistance as shown in Dr. Lammerts lab tests were ample reasons for ignoring it as a parental prospect. It seems little should have been expected if I believed the published parentage.

While WORLD'S FAIR was a Floribunda and consequently not as large a flower as those of the Hybrid Tea Class it was visibly superior in the color of its red flowers to most reds of that class. It came to market during my first year as Director of Research at Armstrong Nurseries. Always searching for varieties to use to "get out the blue" I began using it experimentally within a year or two of its introduction. In those days I knew nothing about "thin layer chromatographic or spectrophotometric analysis" and know little yet except that they are laboratory techniques for separating and identifying pigmentation. All I knew was gained from testing my theories through experimental crosses. I gradually developed theories regarding the types of pigmentation, the visual influence of quantitative levels of same and the effect of one on the other. Dr. Lammerts used CRIMSON GLORY in a variety of crosses while at Armstrong Nurseries and it was stimulating to study the seedlings resulting from them. I had no reason to think that any new genic quality was introduced into CRIMSON GLORY based on the registered cross producing it. However, judging from the results of crosses made with it there was reason to believe that quantitative factors in it for red color were giving to its offspring some improvement in the purity of the red pigment - less blue. By the time I could make such observations some new roses from Mathias Tantau (Kordes' neighbor) were on the market and they piqued my interest. Not much attention was paid to Kordes' BABY CHATEAU in the United States when it was introduced in 1936. However, when Tantau's FLORADORA was introduced in 1945 as an AARS Winner its published parentage did arouse my curiosity. It was BABY CHATEAU X ROSA ROXBURGHII (the Chestnut Rose). No American breeder immediately used BABY CHATEAU but three did use FLORADORA soon after it was introduced.

The published parentage of FLORADORA and its extraordinary lasting quality as a cut flower stimulated experimental crosses by Lindquist, Lammerts and me. By this time I was also influenced enough by the quality of red in WORLD'S FAIR to use it in crosses with FLORADORA as well as with PINOCCHIO and CHINA DOLL. As far as I know only three American breeders used FLORADORA early on and it produced nothing very important commercially for me at once. I obtained EMBERS from the cross of WORLD'S FAIR X FLORADORA. EMBERS scored well in the AARS Trials but did not receive an Award and made little public impression although it occasionally had brilliantly colored red flowers. Unfortunately, too frequently its flowers were dark and burned in the sunshine. In addition the plants were susceptible to Blackspot in areas where this disease was prevalent. More successful crosses involved FLORADORA in succeeding generations.

Chapter 3

ALL-AMERICA ROSE SELECTIONS

One day in the summer of 1939 Awdry Armstrong called me into his office and said that he had just had a telephone call from Harry Marks, President of Germain Seed and Plant Company (later Germain's, Inc.) of Los Angeles. He had told Awdry that he and Fred Howard, President of Howard & Smith of Montebello, California, wanted to come out that morning to discuss the forming of a rose organization along the lines of a flower seed-grower's group called All-America Selections. Their respective companies were members of this group as well as important distributors of roses. In addition, Fred Howard was a world famed rose breeder having bred and introduced the rose LOS ANGELES, and others, with the distinction of having won the Bagatelle Gold Medal of France more than once. Awdry wanted me to be a member of the party which naturally excited me. Thus began the "sprouting of a seed" that was to become All-American Rose Selections, Inc., an organization of vast importance to rose breeders and growers (both commercial and private) all over the world. From this start other prominent growers and introducers of roses were recruited across the United States.

I had an early conviction that vigor of plant was an item that had been neglected, particularly by European breeders of that time. In discussing this with Walter Lammerts I suggested that PRESIDENT HERBERT HOOVER (the rose), then quite new, had merit for breeding purposes because of its great vigor. He responded by crossing it to a McGredy rose named CHARLES P. KILHAM as well as to MRS. SAM MCGREDY, named in honor of the present Sam McGredy's mother. The first cross produced some vigorous seedlings, one of which was voted one of the first All America Rose Selections Awards and was named THE CHIEF (a name Walter used to identify John S. Armstrong, Awdry's father). The cross with MRS. SAM MCGREDY resulted also in a vigorous lot of seedlings and the introduction of a grandchild named FAN-DANGO a few years later - an extremely productive parent in years to come.

Jess C. Watt, Assistant General Manager at Armstrong Nurseries during Dr. Lammerts time there, made an inspired suggestion. It was that Dr. Lammerts cross SOEUR (SISTER) THERESE, a yellow Hybrid Tea from France, with beautiful bud form and color but shy on petals, to CRIMSON GLORY, the best red Hybrid Tea rose of its time, bred in Germany by Wilhelm Kordes. This cross hit the jackpot. One of the first seedlings to bloom had a long slender bud, much like SISTER THERESE but with only eleven petals. We knew the petalage might increase in later flowering stages so the seedling was planted at the head of a row. Walter assigned it the number 36033-1. Our hopes were justified the next spring when it bloomed in the field. It had the bud form of SISTER THERESE still but with the flower form and petalage of CRIMSON GLORY. Everyone at the Nurseries recognized that we had a special rose. I suggested to Awdry Armstrong that it be given the name CHARLOTTE ARMSTRONG, in honor of his mother. She was still living at that time and resisted some but was finally persuaded to give her consent. CHARLOTTE ARMSTRONG won an All-America Rose Selections Award for 1941, giving both Armstrong Nurseries and AARS early recognition as a source of important new roses. Even more important it proved to be the progenitor of an improved race of roses.

While the CHARLOTTE ARMSTRONG rose had many desirable qualities for the garden there were some that it did not have. It was a cerise red and not the dark velvety red of its parent, CRIMSON GLORY. With respect to color the only evidence of its heritage from SISTER THERESE was a small yellow spot at the base of each petal. Dr. Lammerts, knowing the parentage of his new rose, believed he could recover both yellow and red by crossing CHARLOTTE ARMSTRONG to a yellow on the one hand and to a dark red on the other. In pursuit of this idea he crossed CHARLOTTE ARMSTRONG to a very dark red named NIGHT that was also fragrant and rather upright in habit.   One of the seedlings resulting from this cross was very dark red - not quite as dark as NIGHT but certainly much darker and redder than CHARLOTTE ARMSTRONG.   NIGHT was not a particularly vigorous sort but the progeny from it with CHARLOTTE ARMSTRONG was on the whole fairly vigorous.   The new dark red was much more vigorous than the average of its siblings.   It was multiplied, entered in All-America competition and won an award for introduction in 1945.   It had picked up fragrance from its NIGHT parent and also from its grandparent, CRIMSON GLORY for it was very fragrant.   Since CHARLOTTE ARMSTRONG had little or no fragrance, one could assume the probability that the gene for fragrance was a recessive one.   The new rose was named "MIRANDY" after a well known radio personality who talked about garden subjects in the dialect of a "hill-billy" woman. John S. Armstrong enjoyed listening to her over his radio.   An interesting detail about MIRANDY is its changing color as it opens.   The rose is very double with up to fifty or more petals.   The outside several rows of petals are near to the color of NIGHT and the inner rows are nearer to the color of CHARLOTTE ARMSTRONG giving it a two-toned effect on the inner surfaces.   I know of no other red rose with this characteristic.

It is not remembered whether Dr. Lammerts and I discussed a theory of mine having to do with the acquisition of vigor through the marriage of isolated strains while he was still at Armstrongs but it is known that we talked about it at some time.   It seems as though this occurred during one of his visits after 1940.   At any rate it seemed to me that this had happened in the cross of SISTER THERESE X CRIMSON GLORY that produced CHARLOTTE ARMSTRONG and again when NIGHT was crossed to CHAR-LOTTE ARMSTRONG, producing MIRANDY.   I remember seeing the spectacular growth in a hybrid peach population where Walter had crossed a commercial peach of American origin and semi-dwarf character named RIO OSO GEM with a dwarf flowering peach from China called SOOCHOW.   I became very conscious of the possibility of this happening in roses.   Where possible this became a condition imposed on my rose crosses.

Because there are so many different kinds of fragrance and since most of the Hybrid Tea, Floribunda and Grandiflora roses are thought to be tetraploid the inheritance picture concerning fragrance, as well as other character-traits, is complex. I believe there may be modifying fragrance factors - some perhaps intensifying certain scents and others possibly suppressing some. I shall touch on this subject from time to time here as, for many people, this is a very important part of the makeup of a rose. At some time I heard it said by knowledgeable rosarians, "The new roses are not as fragrant as the old-fashioned ones." I believe this a statement of sentiment and doubt that it can be documented convincingly. My DOUBLE DELIGHT a 1977 introduction and one of its parents, Bob Lindquist's GRANADA, a 1964 introduction are two of the most fragrant roses in existence. I have always felt fragrance an added attraction but long ago it became my conviction that other qualities were more important to those who buy rose plants. A common statement is to the effect that the first response to a rose flower is to smell it. It seems more plausible that the sniffer would be first attracted by the appearance of the flower - perhaps its color and form and that the testing for scent comes second. Not many people would be so insistent on fragrance that they would smell every rose they saw regardless of its form and color. The widespread popularity of CHARLOTTE ARMSTRONG, a rose almost entirely lacking in perfume, would tend to confirm this position. It may shock some of those who read this but I cannot remember ever making a cross where the primary objective was a fragrant flower - not even in the crosses that produced SUTTER'S GOLD or DOUBLE DELIGHT. Nevertheless, in evaluating the introductions from my own work it appears that approximately one-half are more than slightly fragrant. There seems to be a wide range of ability in people to sense fragrance. It is my contention that all roses have at least a slight fragrance. I would not argue that in some the pollen may contribute most of the smell. I have assumed in my survey that those varieties reported as having "slight fragrance" were really not fragrant at all for the purpose of my limited survey.

Dr. Lammerts left Armstrong Nurseries in the fall of 1940 to return to the University of California and recommended me to succeed him. For the next several years the responsibility of carrying on projects started by Walter was as much a part of my job as it was to originate new breeding projects. The MIRANDY rose was mostly tested after Walter's leaving and it was not introduced until 1945. While it was distinctive and a great improvement on existing red hybrid teas it did have a flaw that made it subject to early replacement.   An important weakness was in the peduncle (the neck) of the flower which was not quite strong enough to hold the big heavy bloom erect.   In the meantime additional new varieties resulting from Walter's work and from my own were being tested in our screening gardens.

Eagerness to get something of mine into tests led to a careless mistake.   Remembering the first flower observed on CHAR-LOTTE ARMSTRONG, its shortage of petals and its long slender bud, selections were made for first reproduction on the basis of an observation of the buds and not of the opening flowers on a number of seedlings.   Much to my dismay many of these proved to have too few petals, lacked flower form when fully developed and were useless.   This error resulted in unsatisfactory results from many selections in my first year.   It was not repeated.   The next year selections were made for first budding on the premise that if the form of the flower at half to two-thirds open was satisfactory then the bud would also have acceptable form.   This proved to be a correct approach.   It was also discovered that frequency of visits through the seedlings in the selection process was important. With a large number of seedlings it was not always possible to get through the whole lot every day but that was a desired goal.   While a rose flower may last several days in cool weather its optimum stage for viewing will not last that long.   I became convinced the more frequently the seedlings were viewed the more I saw and the more I learned.   Conversely, the less frequently I looked them over the less I found that was worthwhile.

During my first two years as Director of Research at Armstrong Nurseries the additional responsibility of supervising the growing of rose nursery stock was carried also.   After a couple of years it became obvious that it was not possible to do both jobs in a satisfactory manner and I asked to be relieved of the rose production job.   Awdry Armstrong obliged by giving that responsi-bility to another man.   I also asked for a young man from the rose crew to be my assistant.   Homer Dennis' enthusiasm for the job added much to my own effectiveness.   His eagerness to learn was such that he was asking questions about genetics and soaking up knowledge like a sponge.   We often talked about various seedlings -roses, peaches, nectarines, and berries with only their number identification.   At an early state that was the only identity they had.   Awdry Armstrong, as soon as a rose was called to his attention as having special merit, would attach a nickname to it in

19

order to remember it.   That did not help me to remember - it was much easier to remember the numbers.   Our system was to assign numbers to seedling populations in rotation beginning with the first seed planted (usually peaches and/or nectarines which were lumped together).   All seed planted during a given year was identified first with the last two digits of that year.   I continued Dr. Lammerts system which called for the population number to have five digits.   This meant, for example, that the first lot of seed planted in 1936 would carry the population number 36001.   All the seedlings were planted in the field in rows inside a fenced area.   (I had been advised by our patent attorney that our "inventions" must be kept secret until we applied for patents on them.)   The first seedlng in the row of 36001 would carry the additional number 1 and the next 2 and so on, so the whole number in the year 1936 would be 36001-1 and 36001-2, etc.   I used this system as we could easily identify from memory not only the kind of plant (peach or rose or whatever) but the location as well.   It was easier for me to remember them in that way.   I knew at once that a population with the number 36001 was a peach or nectarine and if 36001-1 had some merit we would easily recall what it was and have not only a mental picture of its qualities but its location as well.   This provided me with a language that was the equivalent of verbal shorthand. Nevertheless, I made a typed list of the seedlings and made detailed notes about each seedling considered to have merit.   After a full year of observing the original seedlings I had selected for reproduction and had reproduced all that were felt to have any possible worth I would destroy the remainder.   This destruction is important since if the leftovers are not destroyed they become an obstacle using up space and attention for no worthwhile reason. Again it was remembered that intensity of interest is a great stimulus to memory.   In later years the number identification for populations was shortened so that if it had been applied to the illustration above it would have read just 361-1 and 361-2, etc.

The importance of knowing one's self as it pertains to evaluating seedlings was discovered during my first two years as a rose breeder.   I had heard it said about certain breeders and nurserymen that "pride of ownership was blinding."   This was presumed to mean that some breeders could either not see the faults in their product or disparaged the importance of such shortcomings so they were not seen in the proper perspective.   I had resolved this would not happen to me.   However it was discovered that eternal optimism could also be a stumbling block to seeing things in their proper light. I discovered that seedlings might look pretty good at one viewing and perhaps a second but it must do better than that. In the end a rose must be judged by its consistency of performance - not that it must be at its best with every flower but a majority of its flowers must be worthy. The importance of seeing the flaws as well as the merits in a rose was eventually impressed on my consciousness. This has equal importance in the selection of parent varieties. Not having knowledge of the genetics of many qualities in the rose early on it seemed important to choose parent varieties that complemented one another. By this is meant that where one parent lacked a certain desirable quality it was important to select the other parent that did have it, either visually or with the knowledge that it carried genetic factors for that trait. For example, if one wished to obtain a new variety with glossy leaves it would be unreasonable to choose both parents with dull foliage. Dr. Lammerts had concluded from his work that glossy leaf was dominant to dull - meaning that dull leaf is a recessive pure-strain trait and that any cross between two dull leaf varieties would produce nothing but dull-leaved seedlings. It was suspected that most, if not all, types of fragrance were recessive so that one could not expect to get fragrance in many seedlings resulting from a cross of two non-fragrant parents - at least not very often. On the other hand a cross of two fragrant varieties could be expected to produce a preponderance of fragrant seedlings (possibly all of them would be unless the two parents were chosen with widely different types of fragrance).

In 1940, after Dr. Lammerts left Armstrongs, and being eager to generate something of my own, a cross of CHARLOTTE ARMSTRONG X NIGHT was made - the reciprocal of the one that produced MIRANDY. This cross was made before MIRANDY had been seen so the need for improved red Hybrid Teas was still a priority. It was also made out of the regular season. Eagerness to get started on the project which did not become "mine" until October 1, 1940, (when Walter returned to academia at U.C.L.A.) led to putting some plants in containers under glass. In that way I could make a few pollinations and have some seed at the "tag-end" of Walter's last group and they would carry population numbers beginning with "40." Some of the parent varieties chosen were some of Walter's production that were still unnamed seedlings. One of the first seedlings from my effort was not considered good

21

enough for introduction by Armstrong Nurseries so it was offered to another nursery and accepted. They introduced my "first born rose" under the name of PRINCESS ANGELINE - a cross of CHARLOTTE ARMSTRONG X (MRS. SAM MCGREDY X PRESIDENT HERBERT HOOVER). The pollen parent here was an unnamed seedling left from Dr. Lammerts' work.

The best reds of that day were seriously flawed as to purity of red color and their resistance to Powdery Mildew. ETOILE DE HOLLANDE was probably the best red Hybrid Tea for garden purposes in both respects. The laboratory tests for mildew resistance conducted by Dr. Lammerts did not seem to agree with my visual field observations concerning this variety. I finally determined that the reason for this apparent discrepancy was due to ETOILE DE HOLLANDE's growth cycle - somewhat later (or slower) than most other varieties. This resulted in its escaping infection from other varieties of equal or greater susceptibility. I discovered early that for me ETOILE DE HOLLANDE had little value as a parent. The laboratory index of its mildew resistance proved to have more validity than the field observation when it came to inheritance of mildew resistance. Its offspring did not seem to have any greater degree of resistance than did seedlings from parent varieties that lacked its visual freedom from this disease. As CHARLOTTE ARMSTRONG rated more resistance to mildew than any variety even close to its vigor and flower form it seemed wise to carry on the line of breeding Dr. Lammerts had started. This was especially so as he had not grown very large populations in the time available before he left Armstrong Nurseries.

I was able to secure about two hundred seedlings from the cross of CHARLOTTE ARMSTRONG X NIGHT. The population number I gave it was 40031 and Seedling Number "ninety-one" in that population is well remembered. It was a dark red of about the same shade as the outer petals of MIRANDY. It did not have as many petals and the flower was not quite as large. However, the bud had a more graceful shape and the stems were a bit longer with a neck strong enough to hold the flower erect. Awdry and I agreed that it should be entered in All-America competition after I had enough plants propagated to have observed it several times as a budded plant and decide whether it was as good as we thought earlier. That would have been in the Spring of 1945. We entered several other seedlings from the work of Dr.

Lammerts as well as some from my own efforts. The successful are remembered.

Armstrong Nurseries had been growing several Miniature Roses bred by Pedro Dot of Spain. Robert Pyle, then head of The Conard-Pyle Company of West Grove, Pennsylvania had discovered these when traveling in Europe and obtained an exclusive distribution right from Mr. Dot. Awdry Armstrong had secured a non-exclusive license from The Conard-Pyle Company to grow selected varieties of these Miniatures. He expressed an interest in these to Dr. Lammerts at an early stage in their relationship. As a consequence Dr. Lammerts made a cross of MRS. DUDLEY FULTON (The Evergreen Rose) X TOM THUMB (Miniature) in about 1936. MRS. DUDLEY FULTON was a single white Floribunda with glossy leaves that hung on the plant very late in the season. From that first cross perhaps a hundred seedlings resulted. None were Miniatures. However, one seedling, somewhat more dwarfed than MRS. DUDLEY FULTON, was selected for test. It was a pink flowered Polyantha with somewhat fragrant flowers having twenty-five petals. It is not remembered whether we put this variety in All-America competition but it was introduced under the name of CHINA DOLL. It seemed logical to grow a population of seed acquired by open-pollinating CHINA DOLL in order to test the inheritance of the Miniature trait. This was done in 1940 and about two hundred seedlings were grown from that exercise. It was expected that at least a few would show Miniature characteristics. None did. However, one seedling from that lot did attract my attention. It was a pink Polyantha, somewhat more vigorous than CHINA DOLL, with a softer pink color and extraordinary floriferousness. This variety was put in AARS competition, along with NOCTURNE (#40031-91), but in the Floribunda Class. We named it PINKIE.

In the summer of 1935 Awdry Armstrong had been invited to look over the rose seedlings on the Captain George C. Thomas Estate in Beverly Hills. He went over and took me along. Two or three varieties met with our approval and an arrangement was made with the estate to secure them for test. As remembered only one of these had any importance, but it had great importance as a future parent of other roses. That variety was CAPTAIN THOMAS, a five-petalled yellowed-flowered Pillar with very glossy leaves, quite resistant to mildew. The origin of this rose was given as BLOOMFIELD COMPLETENESS X ATTRACTION. I never saw BLOOMFIELD COMPLETENESS but it is listed in MODERN ROSES 8 as a Hybrid Musk (from Rosa moschata) and resulting from a cross of BLOOMFIELD ABUNDANCE X MME. BUTTERFLY. It was classed as a Rambler. I did know ATTRACTION. It was a rather runty Hybrid Tea but with bright yellow flowers of many petals. It had glossy leaves and while it was not remembered as being especially resistant to mildew neither is it remembered as being particularly susceptible. Captain Thomas (the man) had bred and introduced a long list of "Bloomfield" roses that were claimed to be "hardy." I think that was probably a reference to their ability to withstand the cold climate at his estate in New Jersey. However, I think it may very well have been the Rosa Moschata (Musk Rose) that gave rise to the mildew resistance. Having seen several of the Bloomfield Ramblers and never having seen any mildew on them it seems probable that the Musk Rose was the source of the mildew resistance.

Dr. Lammerts credits me with calling his attention to the mildew resistance of the rose, CAPTAIN THOMAS. His use of it in a cross to SISTER THERESE could be expected to give him a double yellow rose with good mildew resistance in the first generation and indeed it did. From this cross, after Dr. Lammerts departure, I selected a yellow Pillar rose with 25-30 petals that had glossy mildew resistant foliage. The yellow flower was of modest size but the color of yellow was excellent - close to the color of SISTER THERESE. The name HIGH NOON was chosen for it. I budded it in quantity right away and entered it in AARS competition. At about the same time I selected another Hybrid Tea from Dr. Lammerts' cross of MRS. SAM MCGREDY X PRESIDENT HOOVER, worked up a stock of budded plants and entered it in the AARS competion also. This one was a multicolor and a happy combination of the two parents. It was not as tall as PRESIDENT HOOVER but with good vigor, glossy leaves and fragrant flowers. It was named TAFFETA. The introduction year of 1948 found the Trustees of All-America Rose Selections in a generous mood. They voted six Awards and included NOCTURNE, PINKIE, HIGH NOON and TAFFETA in them. The other two were DIAMOND JUBILEE and SAN FERNANDO from other breeders. In their time they were all worthy of special recognition I think but usually the Trustees of AARS were inclined to be more critical. From time to time there were individuals in the organization who tended to try to organize partisanship - not often successfully but occasionally with sad results. When AARS was first formed the personalities in a leadership role of two major introducers of roses from Europe were so extremely different that it caused each to suspect the motives of the other. That fact coupled with Awdry Armstrong's role in leading AARS through its formative stage was no doubt responsible for his election and continuing in the presidency for the first five years.

The Award to the rose, PEACE, for introduction in 1946 did much to unify the groups and was a happy termination to much of the jealous competition. Called "The best rose of the last twenty-five years" by the man who did not have it smoothed some previously ruffled feathers. Another factor bringing about the numerous awards for 1948 may have had something to do with economics. For the two introduction years prior to 1948 only one rose was given an award in each year, PEACE in 1946 and RUBAIYAT in 1947. PEACE was so outstanding in its time that it gained not only prestige for the organization but a good income from assessments on sales. RUBAIYAT, while a good rose, could not hold up the volume of sales established by PEACE so it was apparent to the Trustees that one award per year could not sustain income at a level to support the expenses of the organization.

Dr. Lammerts' success with CAPTAIN THOMAS as a parent encouraged me to continue with this line of breeding and to experiment with other combinations involving it. I was still not satisfied with the intensity of yellow. It would not be inaccurate to state that I was obsessed with getting closer to the maximum intensity in this color. While CAPTAIN THOMAS gave us our best approach to mildew immunity it was noted that when its offspring were reduced to the bush form from the pillar condition of CAPTAIN THOMAS there was a strong tendency to also reduce the number and size of the flowers. While this did not discourage my continued use of CAPTAIN THOMAS and its offspring I was at the same time exploring other possibilities. The idea was to carry along two separate, but parallel, lines of breeding with the expectation of combining them when each line had achieved substantial progress. It was discovered that this approach required a good deal of patience as the ends did not come out even on a time basis. On the one hand my effort was to keep the glossy, mildew-resistant foliage of CAPTAIN THOMAS while improving its flower petalage and size. On the other side the intent was to concentrate on intensity of color and form of bud and flower.

25

In the meantime I did not lose sight of a different approach -improved yellows through CHARLOTTE ARMSTRONG's heritage from SISTER THERESE. I was not impressed with the plant qualities of any of the yellow varieties then available. Being intent on offering more vigorous roses to the public from our program I looked about for prospects that complemented CHARLOTTE ARMSTRONG in as many ways as possible and at the same time were able to transmit yellow flower color. I settled on SIGNORA (SIGNORA PIERO PURICELLI in Europe). This rose had big glossy leaves, was both tall and vigorous, had broad petals and with a better plant habit than CHARLOTTE ARMSTRONG. It seemed obvious from visual inspection that it would carry factors for yellow color. That tended to confirm the published cross which was: JULIAN POTIN X SENSATION. I had admired the intense yellow color of JULIEN POTIN from my days at Coolidge Rare Plant Gardens. SIGNORA had broad petals but that quality would have to be regarded as a bonus since as at that time I had not discovered that CHARLOTTE ARMSTRONG needed a boost when it came to petal breadth. SIGNORA's fragrant flowers also were fortuitous since that quality was not one I was aware of when the cross was planned. Who says luck does not play an important role in rose breeding? Not me!

SIGNORA, as it was renamed in the United States by its distributor, was generally described as "multicolor," although listed in the International Check-list of Roses, MODERN ROSES 6, as an "orange-red" in bud and "orange-apricot turning apricot" in the open flower. This should arouse one's curiosity. SENSATION was a red rose introduced for the greenhouse cut-flower trade. If no other color had been introduced into its parentage then the cross given for SIGNORA would be suspect. So looking a bit further it was discovered that the breeder of SENSATION gave as his cross: HOOSIER BEAUTY X PREMIER. HOOSIER BEAUTY = RICHMOND (red) X CHATEAU DE CLOS VOGET (dark red). PREMIER = OPHELIA Seedling (color?) X MRS. CHARLES E. RUSSELL (rosy carmine). No mention of yellow here although the seedling of OPHELIA could have resulted from a pollination of OPHELIA by some yellow and OPHELIA itself being of unknown origin could have been the product of a yellow variety.

One trait some older European breeders exhibited was to refer to a parent involved in one of their crosses as "seedling of . . ." variety name. When I saw this sort of listing it generated a suspicion that the parent involved was not an unnamed "seedling" but was actually the variety itself. Otherwise why was the other parent of the seedling not revealed. A bit of genetic knowledge would have shown these early day breeders that the result achieved from their crosses could not be duplicated by someone else doing the same cross. As a matter of fact they could not have repeated the result themselves. The chances are that the more important parents of roses bred by and after the turn of the century were tetraploid (with 28 chromosomes) making the list of possible combinations that could be contributed from such parents stretch out almost to infinity. The only thing another breeder could steal from knowledge of his competitors' cross would be an idea. It is my opinion that the selection process (after the seedlings have been produced) may be just as important as the parentage chosen. Furthermore, an astute breeder can look at a seedling and guess the parentage pretty closely anyway. In the interest of history it seems a shame that breeders felt the need to be so secretive.

Since we now know that a cross of a red rose with a yellow or white will dilute the red to pink shaded yellow or white, PREMIER could have carried some genes for yellow and passed them on to SENSATION without it being apparent.

It does seem probable that JULIEN POTIN was one of the parents of SIGNORA and probably SENSATION was the other. If so SENSATION must surely have had a heritage of yellow. As a matter of fact it is possible that OPHELIA may have had some yellow in its background as its parentage was listed as unknown and its color has been described as "salmon-flesh with center tinted light yellow" (a "light yellow" of the era of OPHELIA's introduction would not be very yellow in today's rose language and was almost certainly the product of genes for a different strain of yellow than that in JULIEN POTIN). Anyway it was obvious from the appearance of SIGNORA that it carried genes for yellow color so the cross to CHARLOTTE ARMSTRONG seemed a good way to recover the recessive genes for yellow color from SISTER THERESE covered up in CHARLOTTE ARMSTRONG by the dominant genes for dark red from CRIMSON GLORY. A conclusion was reached that a cross of a yellow with a pure strain red will not produce the SIGNORA color in the first generation. This was demonstrated in the cross that produced CHARLOTTE ARMSTRONG.

A fairly large population of seedlings were produced in 1941

27

from the cross of CHARLOTTE ARMSTRONG X SIGNORA. "CHARLOTTE" was used as the female (seed) parent in this instance. It was common knowledge that some European breeders were convinced that the female parent was the total influence on certain characters and the male on certain others. Neither Dr. Lammerts nor I could accept this with respect to rose breeding. Over the succeeding years thousands of seedlings were grown from this cross and the reciprocal and there was no evidence that either parent dominated any particular trait because of its sexual role in the cross. The first lot of seedlings was searched diligently and many promising seedlings were selected for reproduction by budding on the standard rootstock of the time. It was surprising that no definite yellow ones were found. However, in going through the seedlings one day some dried up yellow petals were found on the ground under one plant and the number of the seedling was jotted down for subsequent budding. No flowers were seen that season as it was late in the summer but ten budding eyes were place in understocks in the field. None of CHARLOTTE's sister seedlings were yellow - most were varying shades of pink. I had expected to find several yellows of the purity of SISTER THERESE in the cross of CHARLOTTE ARMSTRONG with SIGNORA but none were found. However, the seedling under which yellow petals were found in 1942 bloomed in the spring of 1944 and at once it was apparent I had something special. It was multiplied as rapidly as possible and entered in the competition conducted by All-America Rose Selections and the International Trials at Bagatelle Gardens in Paris and in the competition in Geneva Switzerland. It got the top award everywhere it was entered. Awdry Armstrong decided that the name "SUTTER'S GOLD" would be apt as the introduction year was to be 1950, the centennial year of statehood for the State of California. Noteworthy is the fact that it won the James Alexander Gamble Medal for Fragrance many years later. We may assume that this character resulted from a combining of genes from SIGNORA with genes from CRIMSON GLORY through CHARLOTTE ARMSTRONG.

CHARLOTTE ARMSTRONG was in its time a remarkable advance in two ways. The shape of the flower from bud to fully open and the vigor of the plant. It had some shortcomings but none so severe as to discount its flower form and vigor of plant. (The rose breeder must be critical in his analysis of his breeding stock.) CHARLOTTE ARMSTRONG had picked up little resistance to mildew from either of its parents although in that day it was better than most. It had acquired a somewhat ungainly habit from both its parents, it was pricklier than desired, it had no fragrance of flower and its leaves were non-glossy. SIGNORA, on the other hand, had glossy leaves, an upright habit, a fragrant flower and relatively few prickles. SIGNORA did not have very good bud or flower form. Both prospective parents had good vigor and their origins drew from several breeders, widely separated geographically and by their lines of breeding. I had become conscious that the last two facts should have an important and positive bearing on the vigor of the progeny.

The same year the cross of CHARLOTTE ARMSTRONG X SIGNORA was made, a cross of CONTRAST X CHARLOTTE ARMSTRONG was also made, this time using CHARLOTTE ARMSTRONG as the male parent. The objective and the reasoning paralleled the cross involving SIGNORA. CONTRAST was an American product having originated at the direction of Fred Howard of Montebello, California. Its reported parentage is "SEEDLING X TALISMAN" but we were told that the "Seedling" was in fact VATERLAND, a red rose of German origin. The latter information was believable because of a dominant trait contained by VATERLAND and also by CONTRAST. Both had a flower center variously called "cabbage head" or "billiard ball" or just plain "balled." CONTRAST did not have this negative trait as pronounced as VATERLAND but enough to reduce its desirability. Naturally I hoped the fine high-centered form of CHARLOTTE ARMSTRONG would predominate in the seedlings from the cross. I was lucky - it did! CONTRAST had many of the same plant traits as SIGNORA - glossy leaves, upright habit, scarcity of prickles, long straight flower stems and vigor of plant. Again I got many fine seedlings from this cross so I was not disappointed in most respects over the results. The cross was made in 1941 but two seedlings were spotted a year earlier than SUTTER'S GOLD with blooms on fairly mature original seedlings. "FORTY-NINER" was so spectacular that it caught my eye at once. William "Bill" Clark, the Scottish redhead, manager of Germain's nursery division, was with me one day looking at the seedlings. When he saw this one he burst out with "I've got a name for you - call it 'FORTY-NINER.'" We did name it that as it was to be introduced in 1949, the 100th anniversary of the finding of gold at Sutter's

Mill.   (Bill was rewarded with a case of Scotch.) A sister seedling of FORTY-NINER, light red in color and with a flower form to thrill those who show roses was also selected for reproduction.   It was named "APPLAUSE."   (An elderly friend with failing eyesight thought we had named it "Apple Sauce.") Both sister seedlings were entered in All-America Rose Selections competition and in the contest at Bagatelle Gardens, Paris, France.   FORTY-NINER was voted an AARS Award and APPLAUSE won a Bagatelle Gold Medal.   APPLAUSE was the only one of these three seedlings to have non-glossy leaves.   It did have better vigor than FORTY-NINER and better plant habit than either FORTY-NINER or SUTTER'S GOLD.   CONTRAST was neither quite as vigorous nor quite as resistant to mildew as SIGNORA and these shortcomings were reflected in its offspring with CHARLOTTE ARMSTRONG.   Spectacular as it was in color, FORTY-NINER has now pretty much disappeared from commerce as we see today a more vigorous lot of new varieties coming to market.

I think a side-light is of interest.   At the time AARS voted FORTY-NINER an Award it was given unanimous favorable recognition.   The next year SUTTER'S GOLD won a bare majority of the Trustees vote - after two other varieties had won favorable votes with good majorities.   The two varieties voted on favorably before SUTTER'S GOLD were MISSION BELLS and CAPISTRANO both of which have now disappeared from commerce.   The award for SUTTER'S GOLD was sufficiently controversial that an amendment to the AARS Rules was made the following year requiring a two-thirds majority of the Trustees "present and voting" for Award recognition.   Since SUTTER'S GOLD is still in commerce and widely grown not only for gardens but for breeding purposes as well one naturally wonders what happened in AARS.   I think it was a combination of a variety of things that can explain this strange anomaly.   First, there were at that time a number of the AARS Gardens that were permitted to turn in scores in spite of poor conditions.   This put undue emphasis on vigor to the point where only the very strongest even survived in a few gardens.   (Now I believe the Official Gardens of AARS are required to undergo inspection and approval on a continuing basis.)   One garden down-graded SUTTER'S GOLD because of susceptibility to Orange Rust - not apparently generally applicable.   Subjectively, I felt the possibility that Armstrong Nurseries was being penalized for winning eight Awards in the prior three years.

The action for awards in the introduction year of 1951 seemed to strengthen the latter possibility. The first five Hybrid Tea varieties in the scoring were Armstrong entries and they were all voted down. I must confess that only one of these roses was in my opinion worthy of award and it was in fourth place - too far down to be considered. That rose was FIRST LOVE which resulted from a cross of CHARLOTTE ARMSTRONG X SHOW GIRL. It was one of my favorites for many years. It is recalled that at one time I wrote that it was so high in my esteem I hoped to duplicate it in yellow, red and multicolor. However, it had a weakness as a parent that was not noticed until a number of crosses had been made involving it. It had relatively narrow petals and my crosses with it were not very successful because that quality was overlooked. John S. Armstrong was responsible for suggesting the name. It was resisted as too sentimental by his son, Awdry, but "J.S.," as he was known about the Nurseries, persisted and fortunately he prevailed as in retrospect it was a good name. When the variety was used in crosses with roses having broader petals it produced some good new ones. One that comes to mind is PINK PARFAIT, the result of crossing FIRST LOVE to PINOCCHIO.

In the meantime other roses were coming out of the Research Program at Armstrong Nurseries. Some of them were thought good enough good enough to introduce but were crowded out of an offering by Armstrong because of those achieving AARS or other major awards. In the year that APPLAUSE, FORTY-NINER and TALLYHO were produced a sister seedling of the first two, from CONTRAST X CHARLOTTE ARMSTRONG, was sold to Peterson & Dering of Scappoose, Oregon, who named it MULTNOMAH. It was described as carmine with gold base. It had a very long bud that Awdry Armstrong described as "slab-sided," because it did not have flaring tips. Another seedling from the cross of CHARLOTTE ARMSTRONG X NIGHT was also a "fallout" as far as introduction by Armstrong Nurseries was concerned. It was sold to Mount Arbor Nurseries, Shenandoah, Iowa, who named it ROSE OF FREEDOM. WORLD'S FAIR was being tested as a parent during this time because its red color quality was found intriguing. One cross was made with it to CHINA DOLL which resulted in VALENTINE a red Polyantha-Floribunda (I shall call it that as it seemed to be intermediate between the two classes). VALENTINE had a good red color although not as good as WORLD'S FAIR. It resembled PINKIE in habit, similar to varieties produced in later years called "Cushion Roses." I saw it as a very satisfactory intermediate step toward the fine color of WORLD'S FAIR until I tried to use it. It proved to be quite sterile — not completely so but enough to make it very unproductive to use even as a pollen parent. (This reminds me of something most professional rose breeders know. If important enough to use a somewhat sterile rose as a parent then it is much more productive of results if used as a pollen parent. If there is no pollen then surely the variety will not set seed either.) Why should VALENTINE be sterile? I speculated that CHINA DOLL was a diploid with fourteen chromosomes and WORLD'S FAIR was a tetraploid with twenty-eight. At my request Dr. David Armstrong made a study of VALENTINE that disclosed it was a triploid (twenty-one chromosomes) — the normal expectation when a diploid is crossed to a tetraploid. Since the chromosome complement of the sex gametes of a plant are one-half that of the vegetative parts only plants with even numbers are divisible by two without something being left over. As a consequence triploids cannot usually function in a normal manner and are largely sterile. Occasionally a seven or a fourteen chromosome gamete will be formed by a triploid parent and fertilization can take place. Since many more male (pollen) cells are formed than female, if a cross is to be tried involving a triploid variety, it is more likely to be successful when it is used as a male parent.

WORLD'S FAIR was used in other crosses too. One cross was with it as a female parent and MIRANDY as the male. This resulted in two intermediate types, both as to class (between Floribunda and Hybrd Tea) and color (between WORLD'S FAIR and MIRANDY). BRAVO was closer to the Hybrid Tea class and was entered in the AARS Trials as such. It was one of the group of five from Armstrong Nurseries that occupied the first five places in January 1949 when the AARS Trustees decided to vote no Awards for 1951. It was outscored by a more conventional Hybrid Tea from the cross of CHRISTOPHER STONE (a Herbert Robinson origination — introduced by The Conard-Pyle Co.) X CHAR-LOTTE ARMSTRONG. In our climate this did not come up to our standard for color. The first place variety was disposed of to Interstate Nurseries of Hamburg, Iowa who named it BEACON, but were refused registration by The American Rose Society because of the similarity to THE BEACON believed to be still in commerce. Awdry Armstrong decided to introduce BRAVO along with FIRST LOVE, another one of the five.   A testimonial to the influence of WORLD'S FAIR on the color of BRAVO was a remark by Francis Meilland when he saw it growing in our field.   We were walking slowly along the rows of new varieties in our nursery when he came to a stop looking at BRAVO.   I remarked that we were going to introduce the variety but that we wished it were a stronger grower.   Francis looked at me and said: (in his delightful French accent), "But Mr. Swim — the colour, the colour!"   That was indeed the sterling quality of BRAVO.   The sister seedling from the same group was more Floribunda - like in appearance with smaller flowers than BRAVO and not as many petals.   On the other hand it was more floriferous and with excellent color.   It was decided that Armstrong Nurseries had enough varieties to promote so it was sold to Stuart Nurseries of Newark, New York. They named it RED JACKET.

Homer Dennis was impressed at the ease with which he was getting CHRISTOPHER STONE to set seed.   He wondered why we should be using CHARLOTTE ARMSTRONG as a seed parent when it did not set seed nearly as readily as CHRISTOPHER STONE.   He had a good point and after that when a cross between those two varieties was made that was the way we did it.   Since I had little time for the actual physical pollinations his powers of observation were very useful.   CHARLOTTE ARMSTRONG was not the worst seed setter we worked with and it did produce lots of flowers.

Because of its vigor and its superb bud and flower form, my aim, after the Program acquired CHARLOTTE ARMSTRONG, was to cross it to every rose with substantial novelty that Armstrong Nurseries was growing or that we might be able to acquire.   One consequence was to cross it to an interesting Hybrid Tea from Pedro Dot of Spain that he had named DUQUESA DE PENARANDA.   This rose was not very vigorous but I hoped that its origin was far enough removed from that of CHARLOTTE ARMSTRONG so a certain amount of hybrid vigor might be restored to the offspring.   This seed parent was unique in at least two ways.   The flower color was a coppery orange, substantially more stable than that of any other variety in its color range for that day.   I speculated that its color resulted in some way from a mixing of yellow and red genes and that a cross to CHARLOTTE ARMSTRONG, itself an amalgam of red and yellow, might conceivably give us more roses in the color of DUQUESA DE

PENARANDA but with more vigor and hopefully with the bud and flower form of "Charlotte." "Duquesa" also had very attractive foliage - large, dark green and slightly rugose. With this went surprisingly strong, hooked prickles on the backs of the petioles. Only one seedling was selected from this cross, however, and it did not have any more vigor than its mother. It did have two very distinctive characters though. The flowers were a delightful shade of soft but deep pink that kept its color evenly until the petals dropped. It also had the large, dark green, rugose foliage of "Duquesa." If JUNO had retained the vigor of "Charlotte" it would surely have had a long life on the market, I believe. Dr. Von Abrams used it in a cross with one of his own seedlings resulting from GEORG ARENDS X NEW DAWN. Surprising that with all the soft pinks in its parentage PINK FAVORITE was not itself a soft pink. Dr. Von Abrams nevertheless succeeded in two respects where I failed. His PINK FAVORITE had both magnificent foliage and very vigorous growth. I wonder if he tried further to recover the marvelous color of JUNO. Ordinarily I thought of pink as a sort of "throw away" color — meaning that different shades of it were obtained as a by-product in trying for some other color. The shade of pink in JUNO was no ordinary pink in my eyes and was well worth trying to capture in a plant that would give satisfaction in a wide range of gardens. Unfortunately, JUNO did not flower enough to last long. I think it probably has disappeared from all gardens by now. Recall has it introduced by Armstrong Nurseries the same year as SUTTER'S GOLD.

Another cross involving CHARLOTTE ARMSTRONG as the male parent was with MRS. PIERRE S. DUPONT, a rather low growing yellow rose with quite satisfactory foliage. "DuPont" preceeded GOLDEN RAPTURE in availability and was one of the better yellow varieties of its time. Its flower buds were not nearly as well shaped as SISTER THERESE, being short and ovoid but the plant had fewer prickles and was healthier than SISTER THERESE. One of the seedlings resulting from this cross was entered in the AARS Trials, competing against NOCTURNE and TAFFETA and did well but when it did not get an Award it was sold to Interstate Nurseries. They named it ALLURE and described it as "carmine-rose" in bud and "Neyron rose with yellow base" in open bloom. I remember it favorably as it had a much more upright, vigorous plant than MRS. PIERRE S. DUPONT and with longer, more graceful buds than that variety. Of course, I had hoped for some yellow seedlings from that cross but got none of worth.

In the meantime my interest in the possibilities of using the rose, CAPTAIN THOMAS, continued. Either Dr. Lammerts or I had crossed it with a very double rose from Germany named MAX KRAUSE. This latter rose was also large but the yellow color, described as a reddish orange in bud turning golden yellow was actually a rather washed out color when it opened in Ontario, California. It did have fair vigor and the foliage was large and glossy. My principal reason for making the cross was that MAX KRUSE complemented CAPTAIN THOMAS about as well as anything available in yellow Hybrid Teas. It was a convential bush rose whereas CAPTAIN THOMAS was what we called a "Pillar" rose. The flower was not a real clear yellow as was CAPTAIN THOMAS but it had 50 to 60 petals and was large in diameter to overcome the small, five-petal shortcomings of "The Captain." Both had glossy foliage and mildew resistance, especially CAPTAIN THOMAS. My intent was to look at the resulting seedlings, hoping, of course, the perfect offspring might show up. Failing that I expected to make an analysis of the population to see if from it there could be constructed a composite that might "tell" me if I were on the right track. If a favorable analysis resulted I could expand the population the next year hoping that greater numbers might give us a happier combination. If I failed to attain my hoped for goal I must determine if any advance had been made as represented in an individual seedling. If not I again must decide if that cross was worth expanding by constructing in my mind a hypothetical composite of good qualities from all the seedlings resulting from the cross.

Nothing from the cross of MAX KRAUSE X CAPTAIN THOMAS was worth introducing. One Pillar rose from this lot was crossed to a rose introduced in Germany under the name of GEHEIMRAT DUISBERG (renamed GOLDEN RAPTURE in the United States). This latter rose had the best yellow color I had seen but the plant had dull foliage and was not vigorous. Its primary use was as a greenhouse cut-flower variety for the floral trade. I felt the CAPTAIN THOMAS Seedling and GOLDEN RAPTURE complemented one another. I hoped for a pre-dominance of bush rose types and got some. Unfortunately the best flowers were on a Pillar or one that grew so vigorously that it seemed to vacillate between a very strong bush and a Pillar. In our sandy soils it appeared to be more of a bush than a Pillar. Awdry Armstrong was not greatly impressed at first and leaned toward not multiplying it for AARS competition. I kept watching it and eventually persuaded him to allow me to increase the variety and enter it in the Trials as a Hybrid Tea. More on this later.

About this time I found myself wondering "what would happen if." This applied particularly to color inheritance in combinations not previously tried. Historically certain breeders had left their mark on posterity by letting their imagination have free rein. Joseph Pernet-Ducher of France had made his imprint on the history of rose breeding by his experiments introducing the brilliant yellow color of the wild rose, Rosa persiana, into the garden roses of his time. If he or someone with his imaginative genius had not done that work we would not have the bright yellow garden roses we have today. It has been said that "one cannot imagine what one has never seen." Pernet-Ducher's curiosity caused him to bridge a knowledge gap. His contribution of the rose CHATEAU DE CLOS VOGET was credited with the introduction of a vastly improved color in red roses by some authorities. The yellow roses Pernet-Ducher bred and introduced carried his name as a separate class for a number of years with the identity of "Pernetiana." Some of Pernet-Ducher's contemporaries down-graded his new roses with the criticism that they were prone to certain diseases, principally Blackspot and Powdery Mildew. This may well have been true as innovation often brings problems but a negative outlook is not productive.

A contemporary rose breeder suggested an oral agreement that would prohibit me and him from using one another's production in new crosses. I refused to enter into such an agreement feeling that it not only was not in the interest of our respective research programs but was not in the public interest — actually against the spirit of anti-trust. It partly amused and partly irritated me to see breeders who so jealously guarded information about their crosses that they resorted to giving false information to the Registry Office of The American Rose Society. Sometimes this would be in the form of a statement that a new variety resulted from a cross of "an unnamed seedling X an unnamed seedling," thereby avoiding the mention of any named varieties used in the production of the "unnamed seedlings." It was my conviction that it would be impossible to reproduce any given variety by sexual means. It is true that some crosses produce almost an endless variety of good new roses that differ from their sister seedlings. Recognizing this, it still seems to me that the process should be protected —

"freedom of information," again in the public interest. The Plant Patent Law gives protection to the plant breeder for seventeen years on his new rose inventions. It seems greedy to try to get more by having private restrictions beyond the law.

I used one cross over a period of many years and many fine new varieties resulted. The cross was CHARLOTTE ARMSTRONG X SIGNORA previously mentioned as the parentage of SUTTER'S GOLD. Strangely no one else of whom I am aware used this cross although many others used both parents in crosses with other varieties. I noted a few years ago that some foreign breeders were using SUTTER'S GOLD in other ways. I tried it but nothing particularly useful resulted. Perhaps I was unsuccessful because I did not look at SUTTER'S GOLD critically enough. Its flowers do lack substance, the petal width needs a boost and I noted two or three other minor shortcomings. At the time I used this rose in experimental crosses I had neither the variety of roses with good substance (petal stiffness) nor breadth of petal needed —particularly in the range of yellow roses.

Dr. Gordon Von Abrams who bred roses in Oregon some years back identified a gene for yellow color that had the effect of intensifying the yellow more commonly seen. He published an article about it in some scientific publication. Unfortunately his sponsor did not stay in the rose business so the rose world was deprived of Von Albrams' skill.

Mention of Oregon reminds me of an observation that was somewhat disturbing at the time it was experienced. Looking over the roses in Washington Park in Portland in midsummer I noted that the flowers on many of my favorite red roses were burning to a crisp. WORLD'S FAIR which never burns in Ontario burned so badly in Portland that many of the flowers never even opened. I deduced that in that cool climate the flowers developed more pigment making them susceptible to heat absorption. This was one of my first negative experiences with the realities in the realm of red color inheritance. It clearly is not possible to breed roses that have uniform color performance in all areas. Differences in atmospheric content of smog, cloud screen, daily temperature ranges, humidity variances, etc. vary so much from one rose growing area to another and each element has its influence on color, perhaps particularly on reds, that uniform performance in many respects is not possible.

I knew CHARLOTTE ARMSTRONG contained genes for both yellow and red and could transmit these in almost endless combinations. The experience with our crosses of CHARLOTTE ARMSTRONG X SIGNORA, looking at the siblings of SUTTER'S GOLD, indicated that these parent varieties were capable of a wide variety of color transmissions and at the same time keeping vigor at a high level.

I had admired the color of a Kordes rose introduced to the United States in about 1933 called GLOWING SUNSET. It was claimed to be a cross of FONTANELLE X JULIEN POTIN and from my knowledge of the alleged parents I felt the claimed cross was believable. It obviously carried genes for yellow color and I was curious as to the interaction with the red genes from CHARLOTTE ARMSTRONG. GLOWING SUNSET was an orange-apricot with rather long pointed buds but without the flared tips of CHARLOTTE ARMSTRONG. Its colors were rare in that day and they tended to be so fleeting - little stability but highly desirable. I had little idea what might come from the cross of CHARLOTTE ARMSTRONG X GLOWING SUNSET so it was made to find out. A modest number of seedlings resulted from the cross. While I may have selected several seedlings for first reproduction only one was budded in large enough quantity to enter into the AARS Trials. It had a very vigorous plant even though the general level of plant vigor in the population was not more than average. Awdry Armstrong looked at this one seedling on a day when an open flower measured seven inches across. He promptly nicknamed it "Pink Platter." The pink color in the spring was only very slightly tinted with yellow and orange but in the autumn it became more strongly influenced by these colors, blending smoothly with the pink to give a very pleasing effect. Its buds carried the flaring petal tips of its "Charlotte" parent.

Paramount Nurseries of West Grove, Pennsylvania approached Armstrongs for a rose they might introduce to their dealer customers as an exclusive. They were sold a sibling of "Pink Platter" and they named it PARAMOUNT. I thought it a very good rose but it was one more that Armstrongs felt able to market in that time frame. "Pink Platter" went on to win an AARS Award and was named HELEN TRAUBEL.

An interesting genetic happening occurred in connection with these two sister varieties. HELEN TRAUBEL had leaf surfaces that were dull, whereas PARAMOUNT's leaves were glossy. We

38

could deduce from this that GLOWING SUNSET, while having glossy leaves also carried one or more genes for dull leaves. In the case of HELEN TRAUBEL it passed on only the genes for dull leaves and to PARAMOUNT it transmitted at least one gene for glossy leaves. Geneticists refer to the condition of GLOWING SUNSET in such a situation as "heterozygous" for glossy leaf. If GLOWING SUNSET had been "homozygous" for glossy leaf all its seedlings from the cross with CHARLOTTE ARMSTRONG would have had glossy leaves and both HELEN TRAUBEL and PARA-MOUNT would have had glossy leaves. This was more evidence to substantiate Dr. Lammerts conclusion that glossy leaf was dominant to dull.

Only one other seedling from my work is remembered as being in the AARS Trials with HELEN TRAUBEL. It was another Hybrid Tea from the cross of CHARLOTTE ARMSTRONG X SIGNORA with flowers in the yellow range. Unfortunately the color was very similar to one entered by the firm of Howard & Smith. Their rose barely outscored my yellow and was voted an AARS Award. It was named FRED HOWARD after its originator. Awdry Armstrong withdrew our rose from the competition and immediately sensed a "feeling of eagerness in the room" while the Trustees were preparing to vote on "Pink Platter." As remember-ed, the vote was unanimous in favor of an AARS Award for it in 1952. In naming this rose Awdry Armstrong broke his own rule for the third time. The rule was that new varieties should not be named after living people. The naming of CHARLOTTE ARM-STRONG and MIRANDY had already violated this rule. This one was named HELEN TRAUBEL after the most famous female opera singer of the day. She was a neighbor of Awdry Armstrong's at the beach where she rented a house next door to his. She was very pleased when she saw the rose and learned of its AARS Award. Her approval was readily forthcoming.

The next spring after the Award for HELEN TRAUBEL (the rose) was voted, the singer was invited to make a tour of Japan. On learning of this Awdry Armstrong arranged to ship enough plants for a large bed of the rose to be planted in Nagoya. Helen Traubel was programed to sing in Nagoya in early May 1952. It was reported that the bed was in full bloom when she came to see it. The Japanese made quite an occassion of it. The artist who at that time designed and painted all the artistry for Noritake China, in Nagasaki, made a painting of an arrangement of

39

HELEN TRAUBEL rose.   He then had Helen Traubel's (the singer) autograph super-imposed.   She not only wrote her name but added "Helen Traubel -May 7th 1952 - Nagoya."   We were told that just five plates were made and then the mold was broken. The five were presented to Helen Traubel, the artist, Awdry Armstrong, Dr. Ray Allen (then Executive Director of The American Rose Society) and me.   Naturally, I prize mine and I am certain those still living do too.

Armstrong did introduce the seedling withdrawn from the AARS competition, under the name of CHIEF SEATTLE.   We had been informed that it was at its best in the Seattle climate and some influential rosarian of that city suggested a name in honor of the Indian Chief who lived in the area when the white men first came there.   (Chief Seattle, the man, was the white man's benefactor). The flowers of both CHIEF SEATTLE and HELEN TRAUBEL could be classed as daintily colored but the latter was more novel and had a much longer life in the hearts of rose fanciers.   CHIEF SEATTLE had many desirable qualities such as vigor, glossy foliage, fragrance and very fine flower form with 50-60 petals.   The color was just not stable or novel enough to curry favor long with the customers for plants.   CHIEF SEATTLE was introduced in 1951 and HELEN TRAUBEL in 1952.

I became aware of the wide use of PINOCCHIO, a Floribunda variety (from Kordes work), especially by Eugene Boerner, rose breeder for Jackson & Perkins, then of Newark, New York.   My good friend, Bob Lindquist of Hemet, California had used it with FLORADORA to produce LILIBET.   "Gene" Boerner had used it in producing both garden and greenhouse Floribunda varieties. His FASHION, from a cross of PINOCCHIO X CRIMSON GLORY, won an AARS Award for 1950.   I had made a cross of WORLD'S FAIR X PINOCCHIO and from that cross had selected a Floribunda seedling with the precise color of FASHION. Unfortunately, it came a year too late.   I had propagated it for entry in the AARS Trials but did not enter it when I saw FASHION ahead.   My seedling was sold to C. R. BURR & COMPANY of Manchester, Connecticutt who named it ANGELIQUE.   I still have it in my garden.   The flower is not as large as FASHION but the plant is more resistant to mildew with me and is more floriferous.

There always seemed to be rose nurserymen, without a

breeding program, who were hungry for a new rose to introduce and were willing to pay for the privilege. Armstrong Nurseries, from time to time, sold rose seedlings from its research program to such nurseries.

About the same year ANGELIQUE was sold to C. R. BURR two Hybrid Teas were also sold to others. During this period, generally in the early fifties, one rose variety was sold from each of my on-going crosses: CHARLOTTE ARMSTRONG X SIGNORA and CHARLOTTE ARMSTRONG X CONTRAST or the reciprocal of these crosses. ANNETTE from the latter was sold to Earl May Seed Company of Shenandoah, Iowa. It had a salmon-pink flower with considerable fragrance and about 25 petals on a vigorous plant. MIA MAID from the former cross was sold to Mount Arbor Nurseries from the same town. Armstrong Nurseries decided to introduce LA JOLLA, a beautifully imbricated flower of 50 to 60 petals in pink and gold, from the lot of ANNETTE's sisters as well as two Floribunda varieties - EMBERS, a brilliant red from WORLD'S FAIR X FLORADORA and FROLIC, a soft two-toned pink from a cross of WORLD'S FAIR X PINOCCHIO, (both of which are still in my yard).

Having discovered that WORLD'S FAIR had acquired its wonderful shade of red in some way through CRIMSON GLORY, somewhat belatedly, I began using this parent in exploratory ways. One cross was to TEXAS CENTENNIAL from which a Hybrid Tea seedling with pleasing red color was considered good enough to put in AARS competition. When it did not score well enough to put it in contention for an Award it was sold to Breedlover Nurseries, Tyler, Texas. They named it BIG DADDY honoring the head of the Breedlove family. The flower color and plant vigor of this variety were both superb but I felt the flower was a bit small for such long stems and big plant. (I believed that proportions were and are important in a rose. The flower may be too small in relation to the stem length or to leaf size or the reverse of these relationships - both make a rose incongruous to me.)

Dr. Lammerts had made a cross of NIGHT X SANGUINAIRE because of the glossy foliage of the latter combined with its bright red color. SANGUINAIRE also was listed as a Hybrid Rugosa - a fact that intrigued me. A seedling was selected from this cross and named PICCANINNY. It had a five-petal flower, was dark red and the foliage was glossy and that combination in that time was intriguing to me - a rose breeder with ambitions for getting a

41

combination of a double flower of red color on a plant with glossy foliage.   This brought about the cross of CHARLOTTE ARM-STRONG X PICCANINNY.   The result was some pretty good roses but nothing I wanted to put in competition with such roses as LA JOLLA.

Chapter 4

THE GRANDIFLORA CLASS
IS BORN

Earlier I mentioned a seedling I had selected from the cross of (CAPTAIN THOMAS X MAX KRAUSE) X GOLDEN RAPTURE and put through the AARS Trials. Awdry Armstrong had been persuaded to put it in the competition somewhat against his better judgement. At the end of the trial period it was in first place in the Hybrid Tea Class where I felt it most appropriate. When it came up for discussion by the Trustees, as was customary, the Chairman of the Scoring Schedule Committee, who had written me previously questioning the validity of the placement, spoke vehemently against giving the variety an AARS Award "because it was not a Hybrid Tea." Some discussion followed but when the vote was taken it was defeated. I am not certain of the year but think it was for the Introduction year of 1953, the year CHRYSLER IMPERIAL, Hybrid Tea and MA PERKINS, Floribunda were given awards. Our yellow was named BUCCANEER and introduced the following year sans Award. Later controversy rose over the name CHRYSLER IMPERIAL with a majority feeling the name too crassly commercial. The next year the Trustees voted favorably on a motion to require the introducing nursery to obtain name approval. At that meeting one of the more outspoken of the Trustees said, "We made a mistake last year, BUCCANEER should have been voted an AARS Award." He had voted against the Award the year before. By then nothing could be done even if others agreed, as some did, since the variety was already geared for marketing. The problem would not go away as two years later a

43

similar classification objection came up concerning another rose.

Another seedling from the cross that was by now becoming a favorite with me, CHARLOTTE ARMSTRONG X SIGNORA, we thought enough of to patent but backed off from introduction. It may have been a slight improvement on MOJAVE, at least in my eyes, as it was in the same color range with about twice as many petals but we already had achieved the ultimate in recognition with this AARS Winner and could see nothing to be gained by competing with our own MOJAVE. This variety did go far enough that we registered the name BAGDAD for it and obtained Plant Patent #1291 to protect it. These crowded out of our introduction program such roses as GAY LADY, a Hybrid Tea from CHARLOTTE ARMSTRONG X PICCANINNY, sold to Breedlove Nurseries. LOUISIANA PURCHASE, a cerise-red Hybrid Tea, also from CHARLOTTE ARMSTRONG X PICCANINNY and MRS. LUTHER BURBANK from the cross of CHRISTOPHER STONE X CHARLOTTE ARMSTRONG, a fragrant rose pink, were both sold to Stark Brothers Nursery and Orchard Company of Louisiana, Missouri.

The next year another seedling from my star cross CHARLOTTE ARMSTRONG X SIGNORA mentioned above as "wiping out" BAGDAD was actually ahead of its sister. MOJAVE not only won an AARS Award but The Bagatelle Gold Medal and the Geneva Gold Medal — just like its sister SUTTER'S GOLD did a few years earlier. The European medals were delivered to the French and Swiss Consular offices in Los Angeles. Awdry Armstrong saw an opportunity to get some publicity by inviting the two Consul Generals to a luncheon, together with some fellow nurserymen and newspapermen to report the presentation. He got a bargain!

MOJAVE carried Plant Patent #1176. In about this time frame three more Hybrid teas were sold to other nurseries. LEMON CHIFFON from SISTER THERESE X GOLDEN DAWN had a very rich yellow flower with good form but was not a very strong growing plant. PINK FROST from CHARLOTTE ARMSTRONG X TEXAS CENTENNIAL was really an excellent pink rose but it was pink and pink roses were thought not novel enough to enhance the reputation of our program. Both went to Arp Nurseries, Tyler, Texas. SUGAR PLUM from CRIMSON GLORY X GIRONA went to Breedlove Nurseries. It was a very fragrant rose as it should have been with two parents so very fragrant. The fragrance of the two parents were quite distinct in my opinion but in Modern Roses 6 & 8 they are both described as "very fragrant (Damask)." The color was described as "Tyrian rose" which suggests a strong purplish cast and it was not very pleasing in our climate. This was a surprise and disappointment to me as I had hoped and even expected the red of CRIMSON GLORY to be enhanced (made more free of blue) by the red and yellow colors of GIRONA, a seedling of LI BURES X TALISMAN. LI BURES was registered as a seedling from the cross of CHATEAU DE CLOS VOGET (red) X SOUVENIR DE CLAUDIUS PERNET (bright yellow) and had much the same coloring as PRESIDENT HERBERT HOOVER with the dominant colors of red and yellow. SOUVEN-IR DE CLAUDIUS PERNET was one of the most prominent of Pernet-Ducher's early yellows as it won the Bagatelle Gold Medal and was described as "sunflower yellow" — one of the earliest in this color. Unfortunately I did not have a large enough population from CRIMSON GLORY X GIRONA to form a conclusion as to what had happened or what might be expected. What was achieved was certainly not expected nor understood.

About this time several rose breeders saw the need for greater lasting quality in the flowers of the Hybrid Tea Class. It was characteristic of this class in the early fifties to have a somewhat fleeting life span for the flowers. Those who recognized this decided on the same approach to incorporating more flower longevity in Hybrid Teas. Whether this resulted from discussion among us is not remembered but very probably it was as a limited number of American rose breeders were accustomed to rather free conversations. In any event Dr. Lammerts, who by this time was again in private enterprise, Robert (Bob) Lindquist and I had all discovered that the Floribunda, FLORADORA, had substantially greater vase life than any other rose of that era. Vaguely remembered is a conversation with Dr. Lammerts about FLORA-DORA and its cut-flower qualities. Bob Lindquist and I were often "trading" ideas and we both found our discussions stimulating. (It is good to have trusted friends who can try out ideas on one another -not about crosses but about inheritance traits and possible sources of desirable traits). Bob used FLORADORA in crosses to PINOCCHIO and from the seedlings selected a Floribunda that won an AARS Award for 1954. The Howard Rose Company of Hemet, California introduced it under the name of LILIBET, the childhood name of Queen Elizabeth II of England. LILIBET was the companion AARS Winner to our MOJAVE, a Hybrid Tea, the only other AARS Winner in the introduction Class of 1954.

The year before Dr. Lammerts had achieved the Hybrid Tea Winner in AARS with his CHRYSLER IMPERIAL and Gene Boerner the Floribunda Winner with his MA PERKINS. To achieve his Winner Walter made what seemed to me a daring move in crossing CHARLOTTE ARMSTRONG X MIRANDY — a bit of inbreeding, as MIRANDY was itself a seedling whose male parent was CHARLOTTE ARMSTRONG! I do not know what the growth characteristics of this population were but would have expected some general reduction in vigor. If so CHRYSLER IMPERIAL was an exception as it was quite vigorous. Its stems were inclined to shortness and the peduncles likewise. Perhaps these qualities kept the flowers from nodding to much. The red flower color was a definite improvement over MIRANDY as was the shape of the flower — an apparent contribution from CRIMSON GLORY through both its offspring. Gene Boerner's MA PERKINS was the result of a cross of the Hybrid Tea RED RADIANCE X FASHION and a lovely rose it was. Describing its loveliness was a problem as illustrated in the description provided in Modern Roses. There it is "sparkling salmon-shell-pink."

Bob Lindquist got LILIBET into the AARS Trials before Dr. Lammerts or I were able to get any Floradora offspring there. The next year, however, Dr. Lammerts entered a rose in the Floribunda Class resulting from CHARLOTTE ARMSTRONG X FLORA-DORA. I was inspired to make that cross the same year and had a selection to go into AARS Competition at the same time. My rose was red and we entered it in the Hybrid Tea Class. Both roses had flowers with much improved lasting quality. If Dr. Lammerts had entered his seedling in the Hybrid Tea Class I suspect there might not have been another heated discussion about classification. However, it was argued that QUEEN ELIZABETH, the Lammerts rose, was entered in the wrong class. There was a great deal of discussion and it was only terminated when it became apparent there was a concensus that the variety was outstanding and should have an AARS Award and that it should be placed in a special class. The Scoring Schedule Committee was charged by the Trustees with a dual responsibility: (1) to recommend a name for the new class and (2) define the specifications for the class. The Chairman, who was Eugene Boerner, did not want the job and asked me to do it (I was a member of the Committee). Awdry

Armstrong worked with me during the noon hour and by 1:30 p.m. we had no lunch but we had some specifications for the new "Grandiflora" Class and the Trustees were invited to take "pot shots" at both. The Class name was accepted without much argument but the specifications received some discussion and revision. Naturally the class specifications were pretty much a description of QUEEN ELIZABETH's physical characteristics as it was the only recognized member of the class at that time.

A rose of Bob Lindquist's outscored my red entry in the Hybrid Tea Class and was voted the only AARS Award in that class. It was from a cross of CHARLOTTE ARMSTRONG X GIRONA and was named TIFFANY. My rose was not discussed as a motion was made to discontinue voting before proceeding further. Gene Boerner won the Award in the Floribunda Class with his JIMMINY CRICKET from GOLDILOCKS X GERANIUM RED. QUEEN ELIZABETH rounded out the AARS Awards for the Class of 1955. Our red-flowered entry in the Hybrid Tea Class was not immediately reclassified. However, it was later determined by Armstrong Nurseries that it would be introduced anyway and would then be classified in the new Grandiflora Class. BUC-CANEER had been introduced a couple of years before the introduction of either QUEEN ELIZABETH or ROUNDELAY (my red) but since the Grandiflora Class was created before BUCCANEER's introduction it was placed in that class and became the first rose published as a "Grandiflora." This Class carried, as part of its description, "a tall plant with flowers in Floribunda-like profusion but with more flowers with individual stems of cutable length in the clusters." BUCCANEER fit the Class as to height and flower cluster description pretty well in some locations, in others it was nearly a climber.

Dr. Lammerts was then working as the Plant Breeder at Descanso Gardens, at that time a private estate, owned and operated by Manchester Bodie, Editor and Publisher of The Los Angeles Daily News. The new rose, QUEEN ELIZABETH, was introduced through Germain's Inc. It won a place for itself throughout the rose growing part of the world. It was not entered in competition outside the United States but nevertheless won a Gold Medal of The Royal National Rose Society of England, the Gold Medal Certificate of The American Rose Society, and the Gertrude M. Hubbard Gold Medal of The American Rose Society. More recently, at the International Rose Conference in South

Africa, QUEEN ELIZABETH was voted "the most popular rose in the world" (since PEACE was voted such recognition). It has a beautifully formed flower of a soft two-tone pink color about halfway between CHARLOTTE ARMSTRONG and FLORADORA in size of flower. The plant was quite tall compared to any Hybrid Tea varieties then around and had medium sized, glossy leaves, quite free of mildew. My variety, ROUNDELAY, while it did not get an AARS Award did win the Geneva Gold Medal and we thought it well worth introducing. It did not have the consistency of flower form of QUEEN ELIZABETH but it was more double and was quite fragrant with a Sweetbriar fragrance (Rosa eglanteria -the apple-scented rose) and with glossy leaves. Three plants in our garden continue to provide the house with lots of long lasting red roses. Here the color is excellent too.

By this time rose breeders were making crosses of other Hybrid Teas with FLORADORA and the Grandiflora Class became primarily populated by seedling introductions from such crosses. The Class became more and more identified with them. For the first several years existence the Grandiflora Class was represented by some outstanding new varieties. As a consequence they reflected favorably on the Class. When Hybrid Teas were crossed with other large-flowered Floribundas more often than not they were also classified as Grandifloras. This caused the Class to lose some of its distinctiveness, and may have contributed eventually to a loss of favor.

Chapter 5

IMAGINATION IS THE TRUE MAGIC CARPET

-Norman Vincent Peale

Probably the two most important roses introduced between 1940 and 1945 were PEACE and CHARLOTTE ARMSTRONG. These two varieties complemented one another beautifully as I saw it, so as soon as PEACE was in commerce, some crosses were made between them. (It would have been both unethical and illegal to have done it sooner as all test roses were sent out under test license by the introducer. This forbade both sexual and asexual reproduction before commercial introduction.) Where CHARLOTTE ARMSTRONG was weak PEACE was strong and vice versa. "Charlotte" had longer stems, longer buds and more bloom. PEACE had more petal substance, stronger stems, broader petals, larger and dark green, glossy leaves. Strangely not many commercial rose breeders were using CHARLOTTE ARMSTRONG early other than Dr. Lammerts, Bob Lindquist and me. Dr. Lammerts had won an AARS Award in 1953 with his CHRYSLER IMPERIAL which came from a cross of CHARLOTTE ARMSTRONG X MIRANDY. Two years later he won another with QUEEN ELIZABETH from the cross of CHARLOTTE ARMSTRONG X FLORADORA. That same year Bob Lindquist won an AARS Award in the Hybrid Tea Class with his fragrant rose, TIFFANY, from a cross of CHARLOTTE ARMSTRONG X GIRONA. As soon as I thought of it, a cross of CHARLOTTE ARMSTRONG X PEACE seemed so logical I fully expected to obtain many roses from the cross worthy of introduction — to say nothing of AARS Awards and others. Strangely (for I still know not why), out of many seedlings produced from that cross only two were considered worthy of testing through All-America. Only one had early support from me. Eventually that one was put in AARS competition and won an Award for introduction in 1960. It was named GARDEN PARTY and proved to be a winner on the show table when an expert grower got it in his garden. GARDEN PARTY did get its broad petals from PEACE as well as its dainty coloring. Where it got more susceptibility to mildew we can only guess. It did not have the heavy glossy leaves of PEACE nor the long slender buds of CHARLOTTE ARMSTRONG. When well grown it can be impressive with its huge, near white flowers, the dainty pink flush at the outer edges of the petals and its beautiful symmetry. CHARLOTTE ARMSTRONG did lengthen its flower buds some. GARDEN PARTY and its unnamed sister were selected and tested as early as 1952 but they remained in the "Screening Garden" at Armstrong Nurseries until 1956 when GARDEN PARTY was budded for entry in the AARS Trials. A sister seedling with a pale yellow color was kept around for a while also but nothing was ever done with it.

At about this time I had also crossed FANDANGO X PINOCCHIO. This cross was made without any particular expectation. I was curious as to what might happen. It was customary throughout my career in rose breeding to identify the parentage of the prospective parents, whenever possible, by checking in the most recent edition of Modern Roses (the rose breeders' "bible"). The idea was to gain insight into the components of color, functional classification and anything else that might be considered unique and useful in a new rose. Sometimes this was frustrating when I uncovered a rash of "unnamed seedlings" which had neither color nor class identity. I knew from my own records that FANDANGO had resulted from a cross of CHARLOTTE ARMSTRONG X (MRS. SAM MCGREDY X PRESIDENT HERBERT HOOVER). While FANDANGO itself was described as a "turkey red" and "orange-red" with "yellow base" one can discern from this seeming contradiction the variety was a very bright red. An examination of its parentage disclosed such varieties as SISTER THERESE, GOLDEN EMBLEM, CONSTANCE, MME. MELANIE SOUPERT, and SOUVENIR DE CLAUDIUS PERNET - all yellows. Of course there were many other colors involved in FANDANGO's background and that was plain to see without detective work. It was pure Hybrid Tea. We discovered that PINOCCHIO had a much more checkered background. It's parentage of EVA X GOLDEN RAPTURE revealed more yellow which one would expect since the pollen parent itself is yellow. EVA's parentage is somewhat more complex as a cross of ROBIN HOOD (Hybrid Musk) X J. C. THORNTON. ROBIN HOOD is shown as resulting from a cross of an unnamed seedling X EDITH CAVELL. The pollen parent is suspect here as the one given is a Hybrid Tea. A MISS EDITH CAVELL, on the other hand, is shown as a Polyantha. ROBIN HOOD has polyantha-sized flowers and is very unlikely to have had flowers of that size if it were an immediate offspring of a Hybrid Tea. In any event I was curious to test the interaction of our bright red FANDANGO and its hidden yellow heritage with the Floribunda, PINOCCHIO, whose lineage also revealed much yellow. I knew from the prior use of PINOCCHIO by Kordes of Germany and Boerner of Jackson & Perkins that Floribunda varieties predominated in the offspring. My cross gave a spectacular result for that time. I hoped for some surprises and I got some. One was a Floribunda that had a red bud, opened to deep yellow that turned orange-apricot. Of course, I increased it and put plants in the AARS Trials where it went on to win the only Award for 1956 introduction. It was named CIRCUS.

This triumph was not without a bittersweet accompaniment. Another cross involving FANDANGO was also the product of a stimulated curiosity. What would happen if I cross FANDANGO (bright red Hybrid Tea) with FLORADORA (dark orange-red Floribunda)? I made the cross and was thrilled to find one, among the seedlings resulting, that was a truly novel color. The flower was orange-red, of medium to large size and carried the lasting quality of the FLORADORA cut-flower to a remarkable degree. The plants were very vigorous and productive. While some of the flowers formed in clusters the individual stems in the cluster were generally long enough to make suitable stems for a bouquet when cut. The foliage was large but strangely it did not have as much gloss as either parent — obviously combining a predominance of recessive genes for non-glossy from both parents. One could say, almost without fear of contradiction, that the seedling was a "freak." It was a lovely freak, though, and I eagerly increased it to go into the AARS Trials as a Hybrid Tea (The Grandiflora Class was still one year from formation when the entry was made). This rose easily scored in first place but by the time the trial period was complete it was apparent the variety fit the new Grandiflora Class that had been made for QUEEN ELIZABETH the year before. Action was taken by the Trustees to place the entry in the Grandiflora Class before it was voted on.   Some bitter opposition arose at this point and some of our good friends were leading it in all sincerity.   Our supporters were vehement too.   One of the latter remarked: "In three years this variety will be outselling QUEEN ELIZABETH whether it gets an award or not!"   Whether this prediction came true or not is uncertain but MONTEZUMA, as it was named, dominated the show tables in the years following even though it failed to get an AARS Award.   It did outsell QUEEN ELIZABETH for at least some nurseries after the initial three years.   It would seem this may illustrate how some varieties have a strong regional adaptation.   MONTEZUMA did not win an AARS Award but it did win the Geneva Gold Medal, The Gold Medal of The Royal National Rose Society of England, and the Gold Medal Certificate of Portland Oregon.

A similar fate befell another of our seedlings the same year. After the AARS Trustees had taken MONTEZUMA out of the Hybrid Tea Class and put it in with the Grandifloras that action left another one of my seedlings at the top of the scoring in the Hybrid Teas.   After MONTEZUMA's defeat there seemed to have been created some degree of negativism and I failed to get a two-thirds majority for "Big Red" (Awdry's nickname for the bright red Hybrid Tea voted on next).   (I privately referred to the situation as "The 1951 Syndrome!").   This seedling was another and different result from crossing CHARLOTTE ARMSTRONG X SIGNORA.   It was not introduced to the American market but was introduced in Germany by Kordes under the name "MANITOU."   It is unfortunate the the origin was not made available to MODERN ROSES 8, the International Check-List of Roses.   While it was not patented in the United States it was used in further crosses by David Armstrong, but was not available to me.   It had so much to offer — glossy leaves, good vigor, fragrance, 50 to 60 broad petals, bright red color and huge flowers.   Its most serious flaw was its lack of petal substance.   David Armstrong astutely crossed it to some derivatives of Floradora to rectify that shortcoming and several good seedlings resulted.

CIRCUS had real novelty when it was introduced.   It had a weakness though.   The necks of the flower stems (the peduncles) were prone to mildew.   This was not noticed much at first because of the eye-catching novelty of flower color. Again there is a matter of regional adaptability. CIRCUS is outstanding in some areas and flawed in others. After it had been on the market a few years a sport appeared with somewhat larger flowers, stronger growth, and less mildew on the peduncles. The sport was marketed under the name of CIRCUS PARADE. One suspects that there would be little difference, if any, in the way the mildew susceptibility would be transmitted by mother and daughter. A sister seedling of CIRCUS was put on the market under the name of FANFARE. It too had a larger flower than CIRCUS and while it had similar colors to its sister they were arranged a bit differently. Entered in AARS it won nothing there but it did win the Rome Gold Medal. CIRCUS also won The Geneva Gold Medal and the Gold Medal of The Royal National Rose Society (Great Britain). One other sibling of CIRCUS and FANFARE was introduced in France. Someone named it CATHAY. It was not a bad yellow Floribunda. It still grows along our driveway at home after forty years.

Whenever a variety was used in crosses for the first time it was considered important to analyze very carefully the seedlings resulting in order to determine what the parent was giving to the cross that was either good or bad or unexpected. If a variety contributed something important to a cross I felt it useful to cast about in my mind for other varieties to which I might cross it. In a small population of seedlings if the initial cross resulted in a seedling of promise or the composite of the population gave promise then that cross would be repeated on a larger scale. As an illustration, the seedlings from the cross of FANDANGO to PINOCCHIO and FLORADORA encouraged me to enlarge these crosses and to cross all three varieties to others where such varieties had characters that were visually complementary. It is timely to introduce a "ten-dollar" word that is useful — "phenotype," defined as: "the visible properties that are produced by the interaction of the genotype and the environment." (Genotype, referring to the genic or genetic makeup.)

Earlier discussed was the problem of learning the inheritance traits of each potential parent variety given the complicated genetic makeup of garden roses. It was found useful to observe carefully the results in crosses with the aim of evaluating what proportions of a phenotypic quality were appearing in each cross. What was learned was not written down but stored in my memory to conserve time (the wrong thing to do — a misuse of memory). I was disappointed in later use of FANDANGO but was not disappointed in my continued use of both PINOCCHIO and FLORADORA. PINOCCHIO transmitted breadth of petal although it did not appear to have any distinction in this respect phenotypically. It tended to give to its offspring healthy foliage and flowers of regular formation and adequate petalage. It also seemed to give most of its offspring improved lasting quality as cut flowers. When noticed this latter fact was stored away for use later when the variety was used to breed greenhouse cut-flower kinds. PINOCCHIO was the result of a reported cross of [(ROBIN HOOD, Hybrid Musk X J. C. THORNTON, red Hybrid Tea) X GOLDEN RAPTURE, yellow Hybrid Tea)]. ROBIN HOOD was half-shrub (showing its Musk heritage) with red polyantha-like flowers with limited recurrence but extreme floriferousness for a short period. The two Hybrid Teas, of course, had recurring bloom in the conventional way for that classification. PINOCCHIO was used a great deal by Gene Boerner of Jackson & Perkins Co. in breeding Floribunda varieties for both garden and greenhouse cut-flower use. Many award winning Floribundas came from this operation.

It seems probable that Charles Mallerin of Varces, France had been stimulated by Joseph Pernet-Ducher's work as were other European rose breeders. Clearly by using PERSIAN YELLOW (ROSA FOETIDA PERSIANA) Pernet-Ducher had introduced a new color element into garden roses and by the twenties most of Europe had become very aware of it. Such roses as SOUVENIR DE CLAUDIUS PERNET, MME. EDOUARD HERRIOT, JULIEN POTIN, etc. represented such a startling new look that a rose breeder of that time would have had to be extraordinarily ingrown to have failed to see it. Mallerin decided to test the effect of this color element on red roses so crossed one of Pernet-Ducher's, MME. MEHA SABATEUR (described as a deep red with occasional white stripes) to one of his own seedlings achieved by crossing MRS. EDWARD POWELL (crimson) X ROSA FOETIDA BICOLOR (AUSTRIAN COPPER). This resulted in AMI QUINARD. Description of AMI QUINARD in Modern Roses is as intriguing as the rose was "in the flesh" — "Flower medium size, semi-double (17 petals) . . . blackish garnet and coppery scarlet . . ." As a Hybrid Tea it really had little appeal except for its color. The plant was sprawling and the flowers opened quickly and were gone. The color, however, was memorable—the first red I had seen with no evidence of blue. Many roses dating back to that era were introduced with no statement of parentage. Others I remember having similar clarity of red such as K of K, LEMANIA and NATIONAL FLOWER GUILD generally had no published parentage. This is regrettable as I suspect some common thread. Could it be AUSTRIAN COPPER?

Wilhelm Kordes has been impressed by a Hybrid Musk named ROBIN HOOD produced by Pemberton of England. This variety was a shrub with a copious amount of polyantha-size bloom twice a year — bright red with white centers — generally quite resistant to mildew. Likewise, his attention was caught by a Hybrid Tea from Bees also of England, described as "glowing crimson scarlet" and named J. C. Thornton. Kordes crossed these two, achieved a shrub-like small flowered rose and named it EVA. In turn he crossed EVA to AMI QUINARD and a resulting seedling to AROMA. Kordes selected a seedling from this cross and named it BABY CHATEAU. It was accepted in Europe in that day as a Hybrid Polyantha but after Jackson & Perkins coined the name "Floribunda" it was mostly sold in the U.S. under the latter class name. This rose was never widely distributed in the United States and it remained for Kordes' neighbor, Mathias Tantau, to discover the real value in BABY CHATEAU. Tantau crossed BABY CHATEAU X ROSA ROXBURGHI and introduced at least three varieties of Floribunda from the cross. Noteworthy are CINNABAR, KATHE DUVIGNEAU and FLORADORA. These are described in somewhat distinctive terms in Modern Roses 6 and 8. KATHE DUVIGNEAU released in 1942 was described in color terms as "glistening red tinted salmon;" FLORADORA registered in 1944 was called "cinnabar-red," a very brilliant pigment described in Webster's as: "artificial red mercuric sulfide used esp. as a pigment;" and CINNABAR called "vermillion to scarlet-red." Kordes wrote about BABY CHATEAU in terms of a genetic windfall and indeed it was. He produced from it INDEPENDENCE when he grew an F2 (second filial generation —usually from self pollination of a first generation seedling) of BABY CHATEAU X CRIMSON GLORY. Tantau used it to produce SUPER STAR (TROPICANA in the U.S.) and Francis Meilland used it to achieve BACCARA, the most important cut-flower variety in Europe in a generation.

Armstrong Nurseries did not grow nor sell BABY CHATEAU but they did grow and sell FLORADORA and WORLD'S FAIR.

My interest in FLORADORA was in both its lasting quality as a cut-flower and its ability to transmit orange-red color to seedlings from crosses with certain shades of red roses. After seeing this latter quality interest was generated in getting BABY CHATEAU and experimenting with it — especially after reading what Kordes had to say about it. I did not have plants of it, however, while still working at Armstrong. I did have WORLD'S FAIR and it was used in a variety of crosses because the freedom from bluing, as its flowers aged, inevitably aroused curiosity about how this quality might be inherited. One cross, to FLORADORA, had been a disappointment, not because of a bluing of the seedlings' flowers, but because of the extreme dark color produced and attendant burning. It was not crossed to any Hybrid Teas other than MIRANDY during my time at Armstrong Nurseries. BRAVO from WORLD'S FAIR X MIRANDY did build curiosity as to what might happen if WORLD'S FAIR were crossed to other Hybrid Teas.

John Lemon, whom I first knew when he was associated with Joseph H. Hill Company of Richmond, Indiana, had attempted from our first acquaintance to arouse my interest in breeding rose varieties suited to growing under glass for the florist cut-flower trade. This seemed to a neophyte a most exacting market and therefore not worth my time. John was persistent though as well as persuasive. At about the time he left the Hill Company to become Vice-President of The Conard-Pyle Co. in West Grove, Pennsylvania, his persuasiveness had aroused my interest to the point John was asked to give his opinion on the greatest need in the florist trade. At that time he felt the most critical need was in the field of yellow varieties! (It is not believed he knew of my special interest in this color.) The florist industry was at a stage where it was feeling the pinch from labor costs so there was a need for increasing flower production per square foot of greenhouse space. This brought on a trend toward the planting of Floribunda varieties with attendant increase in number of flowers of somewhat diminished size. Growers did not reduce the price to any great extent so growing more productive Floribunda varieties caused income to go up. John had explained this to me so my goal became a better yellow Floribunda. The best one at that time was GOLDILOCKS, a variety with good production but not a very intense yellow color nor much style to the flower buds. Knowing PINOCCHIO's parentage contained GOLDEN RAPTURE and already having discovered its ability to transmit yellow it seemed logical to cross it to GOLDILOCKS. I secured several seedlings that seemed to be possible improvements in color and form. Three or four were selected for test so I talked to Conrad Hartgerinck, Range Superintendent at Armacost & Royston of Santa Monica, California, who eagerly urged me to send him budding eyes for topworking into roses already growing in their benches. In a couple of months he telephoned reporting excitedly that one of the topworked seedlings had real promise. He asked if I could field-bud enough plants to fill at least half a bench — about two hundred roses. His suggestion was to send the plants as "dormant eyes" (budded but not forced out) which I did. In another two or three months I was invited to come over to see the plants in bloom. From that beginning this new yellow "Sweetheart" (the class name in the florist trade) was soon introduced to the industry through Carlton Rose Nurseries and was named GOLDSTRIKE. This was the only florist cut-flower rose to be bred at Armstrong Nurseries for many years.

Chapter 6

A NEW ENTERPRISE

CIRCUS was given an AARS Award while I was still at Armstrong Nurseries but introduced after my departure and a new firm formed in the shape of a partnership with O. L. Weeks of Ontario, California. The new company was to operate under the name of SWIM & WEEKS. After fifteen years as Research Director at Armstrongs it was discovered that more and more I was becoming involved in administrative matters that took away time from plant breeding. A wish to continue rose breeding was strong enough to inspire a drastic change at forty-eight years of age. Mr. Weeks, whom I had always known as Ollie (pronounced Olie), had for a number of years operated Week's Wholesale Rose Grower as a solely owned nursery supplying nursery-grown roses to retail dealers. Fortunately for me Ollie also wished to become involved in a new and fascinating profession and business. I had known him for many years in the relationship of a licensee of Armstrong Nurseries' patented roses and was aware of his integrity.

All of the rose breeders in California had made their crosses on plants in the ground or in containers, and in the open air. There had been a brief exception. When Dr. Lammerts initiated the rose breeding program at Armstrong Nurseries he was supplied with a small greenhouse in which to carry on various operations requiring an environment for growing small seedlings of both roses and fruits. In order to get started quickly he put a few parent plants in five-gallon containers in the greenhouse, brought them into flower and pollinated them there. I remembered that hips (seed pods) set readily under these conditions and decided to start the SWIM & WEEKS operation in the same way. This involved building a new greenhouse, as none was available otherwise. The partnership had leased office space from Ollie and it was decided to build the greenhouse nearby also on land leased from him. That made it easy for me to scoot back and forth from the office to the greenhouse. My office was a converted chicken brooder house on Ollie's home property. (He had bought the property from a poultryman.) The office complex consisted of an office of comfortable size with a desk and chair, a typewriter (for me) and two four-drawer filing cabinets. In another room behind my desk was a bathroom with toilet, lavoratory and shower. Adjacent to that was a room that could be closed off with a sliding door in which we kept a refrigerator. All of this was on a cement slab which meant that any room without heat would stay cool and the room with the refrigerator was not heated. This room was ideal for parking the newly harvested pollen overnight.

Ollie had not made pollinations of any sort before and wanted to learn as he expected to help me as much as time permitted. The first step was emasculation (removing the anthers) of each flower just before it opened. The timing varied with each variety but the need was to remove the anthers before they burst and started to shed pollen. Varieties with few petals had to be emasculated at an earlier stage than many-petaled ones. It was discovered that a very dark red variety, BABY CHATEAU, needed to be worked on at an earlier stage than other sorts. Otherwise it shed pollen while the flowers were still in the bud stage. (Further comment on this later.) The first step was to remove all the petals. I removed not only all the petals but the sepals as well. I found the latter just got in the way and served no useful purpose. Different breeders have different methods of marking the flowers after emasculation. Some leave a single petal until after the flower is pollinated, some leave a single sepal as a marking device, etc. I used colored marking tags on which I wrote the date of emasculation. Our cross list was made up before we started any of this work and each cross on each seed parent was assigned a color of tag. In order to use all the pollen and make full use of our plants and space each variety served as both male and female. In other words if I were crossing CIRCUS X QUEEN ELIZABETH I would also cross QUEEN ELIZABETH X CIRCUS (the first named in all instances is the female (seed parent) and the second is the

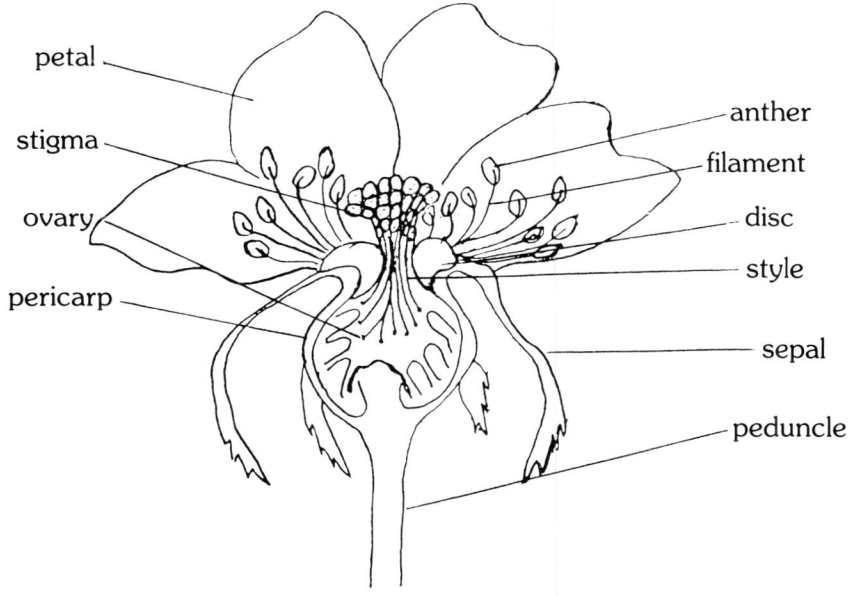

petal

stigma

ovary

pericarp

anther

filament

disc

style

sepal

peduncle

Cross-section diagram of a simple rose flower with one or two rows of petals. See Pages 60 and 62 and the "Adder dum" by Dr. Walter E. Lammerts at the end of this book for explanation of the role of these parts. The "pericarp" becomes the "hip" (seed pod) when ripe. The "disc" is the upper end of the pericarp. Attached to it, progressing inward, are the sepals, petals and stamens. The stamens are the male part of the flower. The stigmas, styles and ovaries are the female parts and together compose the "pistils."

male (pollen parent).   After the petals were removed the anthers, each on a filament (thin stalk), were usually found arranged in a loose circle around the pistils and stigma.   Since these parts are differentiated leaves there are fairly frequent occasions where the filaments and anthers are mixed with the pistils and stigma in a confused pattern.   All the anthers must be removed to prevent self-pollination and this may be somewhat tedious where the sexual parts are mixed.   I used a knife of modest size with a blade broad enough to push several anthers gently against it with my thumb and pulling them away from the filaments then depositing each load in a small, clean, sterile cosmetic jar, with a white painted lid on which I could write, with a lead pencil, the variety name of the anthers.   In the event of a disordered mix of stamens and pistils I found it useful to have a pair of tweezers to separate out the anthers.   In any event a combination of knife and tweezers were appropriate pieces of equipment.   I found it advisable to put no more than three quarters of an inch of anthers in the bottle before I took it to our cool room and emptied it on a clean sheet of white typing paper.   (There is a tendency for the anthers to sweat if too many are in the bottle at one time.)   Overnight the anthers would burst and shed their pollen so they could be scooted back in the jar from which they came and be ready for pollinating the flowers emascu-lated the day before.   If I did not have the right pollen to use as soon as a female variety was ready overnight I could pollinate as much as three days after emasculation.   I followed the practice of putting small paper bags over the emasculated flowers to avoid the possibility of an insect bringing pollen from an unwanted source. This was probably not necessary as I found insects (bees, at least) were not interested in a flower that did not have its pollen.   Our method of getting pollen from the jars to the pistils of the rose to be pollinated was by means of an artist's small paint brush.   I learned that pollen began losing its viability after about twenty four hours.   However, this did not cause me to throw it away that soon.   There seemed to be some degree of viability on most varieties up to three days.   It is suspected that the weather had much influence on this factor.   If it were hot the pollen had a shorter life than if it were cool.   I kept a chart of our crosses in the greenhouse where I could record the number of emasculations for a given pollination and the date on which they were pollinated.   As far as the price tags on the plants were concerned I penciled a big "X" on it when the job was complete.

I removed the bags from the crosses after about three weeks in order to watch the condition of the hips. It was discovered that some varieties were more subject to rot than others. A chemical solution to this problem had not been found at that time. I knew it was worse when the humidity was high. My solution was to leave the top vent of the greenhouse open a few inches at night when the heat would carry the excess moisture out the vents. This seemed to work fairly well although I always seemed to lose hips on some varieties even then.

I started our pollinations about April 1 and discontinued about June 1. I liked to let the hips have six months of ripening — if they would stay on that long without rotting. Normal ripening would see them turn deep golden yellow or red and sometimes some varieties would russet on top of these colors. We had no cooler for our seed greenhouse other than side and top vents so daytime temperatures during many days in the summer would range from 90 to 100° Fahrenheit. This dried out the soil in the cans rapidly so it was necessary to water every day during the seed ripening process unless some cool days intervened. Sometimes after a hip seemed to be set the peduncle to which it was attached would turn yellow and a day or two later that changed to brown. If the hip had been formed for as long as four months it would be harvested, the seed removed and put in a pan of water to which a small amount of surfactant had been added. Any seed that floated was thrown away and the ones that sank were saved for planting. (The seed that floated rarely had a viable embryo.) The seed was planted in square flats made of redwood about three inches deep. The planting mix was composed of one-third sharp sand, one-third peat moss and one-third sandy loam soil. Prior to planting this was thoroughly mixed and then fumigated with methyl bromide (supplied in pressurized canisters by a chemical company) to destroy any nematode, allowing it to remain under an air-tight tarpaulin overnight and then aired for three days before seed planting.

The seed flats measured sixteen inches square which permitted two rows on each side bench. A hand press was constructed to fit inside the flats, about three inches thick with two hand grips on one side and 169 broad-headed tacks (13 x 13) driven in at regular intervals and at the same depth on the other side. This was designed so that, when inserted with the tack side down, pressure could be applied to the soil mix by grasping the hand grips and putting one's weight on it. This would leave depressions in the planting medium in which seed could be planted at regular intervals, one seed to a hole. The holes were about ⅜ths inch deep. After the seed was dropped in the holes enough planting medium was placed over them to bring the surface to level and the medium thoroughly watered — slowly with a fan-type spray head, until water ran out the drain holes in the bottom of the flat.

As related earlier, the bulk of the seed was harvested as it reached six months of age on the plant (from pollination date). The hips were placed in aluminum pans (or any type of open container) and left in the cool room in our office complex. The seed was removed from the hips within a very few days, put in paper bags, liberally sprinkled with Captan, then into the refrigerator which was kept at about 40° F. As soon as harvest had been completed for a given cross I planted the seed. As I had done before I gave the first population (cross) a number beginning with the last two digits of the year in which the seed was planted, followed without interruption a numbered identification for the population i.e. for that year the first population would be 551, the next 552 and so on. This information was entered in a looseleaf notebook and on a wooden label tacked to the front top edge of the seed flat. In the notebook not only the population number was entered but the identity of the cross and the date the seed was planted. Later as seedlings came up and were transplanted the quantity of each transplanting was entered in the notebook.

It had been so long since this type of operation had been done I was unable to predict specific times for germination to take place. In addition many of the seed parents were different than they had been in 1940, fifteen years earlier, and each seed parent gives its offspring a different "timeclock" for germination. Some fretting took place on my part when, after six weeks, nothing had appeared to break the surface of the seed flats. My family were accustomed to lease a house from a friend for a couple of weeks on Balboa Island just before school began for our girls. Ollie and Verona Weeks suggested I go down there to be with them probably sensing that my worrying would not cause the seed to germinate any faster. After two or three days on "The Island" a telegram came from Verona announcing the "birth" of the first "rose baby" with promise of additional ones appearing soon. Some relaxation set in then - probably accompanied by sleep. By the time the vacation was over quite a scattering of seedlings had appeared.

The spacing of the seed in the seed flats was designed so that a transplanting tool made for us could remove each seedling from the flat with a cylinder of soil about the roots and not disturb the soil around the adjacent seed. As the seedlings came up the first thing that appeared were the cotyledons (seed leaves). From between these soon came a stem with true leaves on it. My practice was to transplant the seedlings as they acquired three true leaves. At that time I had just been "introduced" to the use of a pot made of peat. I found this fit my way of doing things very nicely as the roots of the rose seedlings could grow through the walls of the pot and be transferred to the field without removal from the pot. It had been my practice, as it had been that of Dr. Lammerts before me, to plant all original seedlings in the field and make our garden rose selections under those conditions. For a while Bob Lindquist followed this practice but I think he discontinued it near the end of his rose breeding career. The California operation of the Jackson & Perkins Company was handled in this manner but in Newark all the initial selections were made under glass. As that company was seriously involved in breeding greenhouse cut-flower roses this was a natural way of handling the seedlings. I confess to an inability to select garden roses in the greenhouse. The character traits observed under glass were not the same ones appearing in the field or garden and it never became apparent to me how they could be translated. Perhaps the most important single trait as I saw it was consistency and I could not measure garden roses for this under greenhouse conditions.

Chapter 7

DISASTER AND RECOVERY

The use of a greenhouse for producing seed at Swim & Weeks in a rose breeding operation did not go unobserved by other breeders in Southern California. Neither Dr. David Armstrong at Armstrong Nurseries nor Robert Lindquist at Hemet Wholesale Nurseries in Hemet, California had previously set seed under glass. However, within a year of our first seed harvest they had each built greenhouses for that purpose. It should be pointed out that, while the use of a greenhouse is a more efficient way of setting seed, it probably is not practical for the amateur who cannot or does not wish to go to this expense or who does not have space. Neither Dr. Lammerts nor I used a greenhouse at Armstrong Nurseries from 1935 through 1954 for this purpose. We did use a greenhouse for germinating the seed and growing the seedlings and it would have been a handicap to not have had one for this purpose. However, it can be done with a screen-house satisfactorily.

Swim & Weeks built a second greenhouse in which to set seed and used the first one to grow the seedlings. I had planted mother plants in the ground to establish them for setting seed the second year but when I had such success in 5-gallon containers under glass I dug them all up. I knew from experience that most rose varieties will not set seed very well in their first year of growth after transplanting to the ground. Plants intended for such use should not be pruned in the usual way. Only dead wood and hips should be removed during the dormant season. It is not impossible to set seed in the first year of growth but is easier to do so if the plants are grown in containers. Growing the plants in containers does require a degree of diligence with respect to watering. They must not be allowed to get excessively dry as that will stop the maturing of hips. They will dry up. One day in a wilt and a season's pollinations are for naught. For this reason regular and periodic watering is as necessary in the ground outside as it is in a greenhouse - less of a problem when the plants are in the ground but there is a trade-off. Seed does not set as readily in the first year when the mother plants are in the ground. At the end of the first year in the ground the plants should not be pruned except for removing dead wood and volunteer hips and old flowers. Hips will set more readily the second year and the rose blooms used as pollen parents will yield more pollen and more viable pollen. Most such practical techniques I learned in the "school of hard knocks" but this truth was learned as a Horticulture student in college. At that time we were taught that fruiting plants (rose hips are fruit) in their vegetative stage need an abundance of Nitrogen but when they become adult enough to bear fruit there needs to be a balance of Nitrogen and Carbohydrates. Hard pruning tends to put a strong growing rose back into a vegetative state for at least the first bloom. If it is a strong growing variety hard pruning may make the plant too vegetative to set seed for two periods of bloom. It was my experience that the first bloom period, when seed production is carried on in containers, gave us the most satisfactory seed set because the hips had progressed enough in their maturity by the warm weather of summer that they hung on more reliably and the germination percentage was likewise better. Dr. Von Abrams in Scappoose, Oregon experienced considerable difficulty in maturing seed on mother plants outside and discovered that it was for lack of heat during the maturation period. He was kind enough to send me a reprint of his paper about the relationship of temperature during seed maturation to subsequent germination. In Southern California I did not have to contend with the cool climate of Oregon. Our climate was near ideal for seed setting. While aphis and spider mites were common pests I had reasonable controls for them even then. Powdery Mildew could be a problem and to a lesser extent Rose Rust. Blackspot was rarely seen in our particular area at that time. Over the last few years and with wide movement of plants around the country an increasing amount of Blackspot is seen. There are effective chemical controls of all three of these diseases and it is most important that rose breeders control them on their mother plants. It is gratifying to note that there continues to be improvement in the resistance to all three diseases in the better new varieties coming to market recently.

One pesky problem I had was related to cetain parent varieties. Damping-off was generally pretty well controlled by the liberal use of Captan sprinkled on top of the seed flats. However, Captan seemed to be rather ineffective in controlling an affliction resembling damp-off of seedlings having PINOCCHIO as one parent. I came to the reluctant conclusion that something in the genetic makeup of PINOCCHIO as well as certain cther Floribunda varieties (most of them related to PINOCCHIO) were responsible for this quasi-damp-off. This did not stop me from using PINOCCHIO - just made it more difficult.

Dr. Lammerts followed the practice of planting his rose seed in seed flats immediately after harvest. Such seedlings as germinated by the end of the calendar year were potted and grown on under glass until it was warm enough outside that they would be able to continue growth after transplanting in the field. Much of the seed did not germinate during the calendar year and were transported to cold storage in the seed flats where they remained at 34°F. for ninety days. They were watered thoroughly before being taken to cold storage and needed no further watering while there. On being brought out of storage into the greenhouse there began heavy germination for a few weeks and the seedlings were potted as they attained three true leaves. In about six weeks after potting each seedling would have a bloom - usually about one-third to one-half the size it would become at maturity. Petal count would vary considerably in relation to what it might become at maturity. As related earlier, CHARLOTTE ARMSTRONG had only eleven petals in that first bloom but at maturity had about thirty five.

As Dr. Lammerts was my mentor I followed the same routines at Swim & Weeks - with one major exception. Ollie Weeks was so impressed with the wealth of germination that occurred after the cold storage treatment he suggested I put the seed flats in cold storage immediately after planting. This seemed like a reasonable suggestion so I did. Armstrong Nurseries was using the same commercial cold storage in which to store budding eyes. As the management at the cold storage plant had been told the temperature at which we wished to store the seed the prior year it may not have been repeated the second year. It was not discovered until the seed flats were being removed at the end of ninety days that they had been stored at the same temperature as Armstrong's budding eyes - 28 to 29° F. The seed flats had ice encrusted on top of the soil-medium. My heart sank. This was a new experience and I did not know what to expect but was fearful as had heard that rose seed did not react well to freezing. This lot did not germinate well. Just how much the frost contributed and how much the lack of after-ripening had to do with it was never discovered as the next year I returned to the routine followed the first year. In retrospect it is believed the real damage occurred when the after-ripening that occurred the previous year in the seed flats in the greenhouse was skipped in this second crop. It was apparent that my effort to get off to a good start had suffered a major setback in the second year. Out of over 50,000 seed planted only about 2,000 seedlings were strong enough to transplant to the field. (Our standard practice was to eliminate before potting those seedlings exhibiting substantial inherent weakness or susceptibility to mildew and that practice was not changed because of the disaster.)

Dr. David Armstrong, who succeeded me as Director of Research at Armstrong Nurseries in 1955, was faced with the same types of problems that Dr. Lammerts left with me - preserve anything of value started by his predecessor and at the same time start his own program. Such varieties as MONTEZUMA, CIRCUS and GOLDSTRIKE had already gone through the test period, including AARS for MONTEZUMA and CIRCUS before I left, but were introduced to the trade after Swim & Weeks was started. GOLDSTRIKE and MONTEZUMA were introduced in 1955 together with WILDFIRE, (another red-flowered Floribunda with five-petal flowers from the cross of WORLD'S FAIR X PINOCCHIO with the fine color quality of its mother, WORLD'S FAIR.) CIRCUS was not introduced until 1956 along with its sister FANFARE. Two other somewhat curious varieties were introduced by Armstrong that same year. MIDNIGHT, a very dark red and a very vigorous Hybrid Tea from a cross of GAY LADY (CHARLOTTE ARMSTRONG X PICCANINNY) X TEXAS CENTENNIAL. The chief character of interest in this variety was its very dark red color, which inspired the name, and the fact that the color stayed much the same throughout the life span of the flowers. Most very dark red varieties have a tendency to be black in the initial stage of the flower bud and inasmuch as black absorbs light the petal temperature rises enough to scorch and ruin the flower. The flowers of MIDNIGHT avoided this

70

problem just as did its forbear, PICCANINNY, which in turn was believed to acquire the trait from NIGHT. It also acquired the glossy foliage of PICCANINNY and fragrance from its whole parental line, perhaps especially from TEXAS CENTENNIAL. The other curiosity was a Floribunda from a cross of SUTTER'S GOLD X ONDINE. As both parents were Hybrid Teas it was indeed curious that MOONSPRITE was a Floribunda with cream colored flowers. The possibility of an accident occurring that might have caused the seedling to be misplaced seemed probable but no one could construct a plausible cross to cover the situation. The kind of rose represented in MOONSPRITE was, to say the least, an aberation and fit no pattern of inheritance with which I was familiar. One other rose introduced in 1956 from a cross and selection made by me was FORT VANCOUVER resulting from a cross of CHARLOTTE ARMSTRONG X TIMES SQUARE (MRS. SAM MCGREDY X PRESIDENT HERBERT HOOVER). FORT VANCOUVER was introduced and sold by Peterson & Dering of Scappoose, Oregon. Awdry Armstrong felt it to be a good rose but as it was a pink Hybrid Tea was not distinctive enough to justify introduction in the program at Armstrong Nurseries.

In 1957 Dr. Armstrong and his father Awdry chose two seedlings to introduce to the American nursery trade that resulted from my crossing and testing. STARLET was a Floribunda from the general family of crosses aimed toward new yellow forcing "Sweethearts" (Floribunda-Polyantha). Its parentage was GOLDILOCKS X (FANDANGO X PINOCCHIO). The name of the pollen parent was not published but vaguely it is remembered as CATHAY (FANDANGO X PINOCCHIO). CATHAY was put into the Bagatelle Trials and eventually introduced in France and used by me to some extent in my breeding effort as it was the best pure yellow to result from the cross that produced it. It seems the name was not registered for CATHAY at the time the name for STARLET was registered with The American Rose Society. If it had been I think CATHAY would have appeared as the pollen parent of STARLET. This did not apply to the registration of the parentage for MANITOU and we do not know why the parentage was not registered unless Kordes applied for registration of the name and not knowing the parentage did not inquire. Since I remember the rose very well it is recalled the parentage was CHARLOTTE ARMSTRONG X SIGNORA - another in the long line of significant roses from this cross.   The other rose introduced in 1957 to the American garden trade was AZTEC, selected by me but introduced after I was gone.   AZTEC was another seedling of CHARLOTTE ARMSTRONG but the other parent was not given to the registry but shown as an "Unnamed Seedling." I do not recall what produced the Unnamed Seedling but a guess would have it as MONTEZUMA for one parent.   That would be believeable.   If so AZTEC would represent a reversion to the habit of CRIMSON GLORY (its grandparent and greatgrandparent) as it was spreading and had the somewhat curved necks (peduncle) of that variety. Its color was much deeper and richer than MONTEZUMA but in the orange-red range.   The plant habit and the weak peduncles were the worst faults but even so it made a big impression in Australia when it reached there.   There was some regression in vigor as one might expect would result from inbreeding as represented by my guess as to the cross.

Chapter 8

GOOD NEWS — A NEW OUTLET

In 1955, it seems, I had a letter from Sidney B. Hutton, Sr., President and Chairman of the Board of The Conard-Pyle Co. of West Grove, Pennsylvania that was to have great significance for Swim & Weeks. The essence of the letter was to the effect that The Conard-Pyle Co. would be interested in testing our new seedlings with a view to obtaining an option to purchase those that survived the test of approval from their key people. Mr. Hutton pointed out that his company did not have a breeding program of its own but relied on several outside sources to supply the new introductions of their firm. I knew The Conard-Pyle Co. had exclusive American distribution agreements with some European breeders. One of the more important of these was with Francis Meilland of Cap d'Antibes, France, the breeder of PEACE and many other world renowned roses. Charles Mallerin was another of their famous suppliers. At the time of my letter from Mr. Hutton, Swim & Weeks had not begun making selections from the first year's crop of seedlings so there were no specific new roses about which we might be thinking of plans for introduction. I already had an agreement with Weeks Wholesale Rose Grower under which Ollie had the right of first refusal on any rose produced by Swim & Weeks. Under the circumstances the appropriate reply to Mr. Hutton's letter must be determined by Ollie. He was not one to "burn bridges" so Mr. Hutton was encouraged with my approval to submit a proposal for us to consider. Just what Ollie had in mind is not exactly remembered but it seemed probable to me at that time that he would introduce through Weeks Wholesale Rose Grower our best output - hopefully AARS Award Winners. We could have had no idea how many worthwhile new roses might come from the program nor how fast they might appear.

Negotiations ensued over the next year and a half. We had visits from Sidney B. Hutton, Jr., a then Vice-President of The Conard-Pyle Co. and from John Lemon who had left the Joseph Hill Company to join The Conard-Pyle Co. as another Vice-President. They both wanted to look over our output up to that time and to carry discussions further. Sidney, Sr. had told us the type of financial arrangement they had with their European suppliers. This seemed generally satisfactory but the final testing, option and purchase agreement must have taken at least one and a half years to complete. It was decided that we would send The Conard-Pyle Co. test plants of each variety we entered in the AARS Trials so they might judge them in their screening garden at the same time they judged them in their official AARS Garden. Mr. Hutton was at that time an Official AARS Judge but could not judge (officially) any variety in which his company had a financial interest, according to AARS Rules.

The first seedlings sent them were our first two entries in the AARS Trials. As the first seedlings germinated they were potted successively to two-inch peat pots, four-inch clay pots, and six-inch clay pots - all under glass. By the time the weather got warm enough to transfer the seedlings to the field in 1956 some of the earliest transplantings were a foot or more in height. As a consequence I was able to begin making judgements as they came in bloom in the field. Three seedlings were selected for multiplication, one Hybrid Tea and two Grandifloras. All three were cut as hard for budding eyes as the original plants would permit, the eyes budded to our standard rootstock (by then, DR. HUEY) and the eyes forced into growth as soon as they were "stuck" by notching the understock one-quarter inch above where the budded eye was placed and breaking it over but leaving the understock top attached. Leaving the understock attached gave much added impetus to the growth of the bud that we wanted to hurry. The intent was to take additional budding eyes from the forced ones and to so increase the numbers. (I had learned this technique from Frank Raffel, proprietor of Port Stockton Nursery in Stockton, California who used to ship plants with this "nurse" attached, for an extra price.)

74

I eliminated one of the Grandifloras after the second bloom. It had an unusual rusty orange color but the flowers were judged to be too small in proportion to the length of the stems and the size of the plant. The Hybrid Tea was from my favorite cross - CHARLOTTE ARMSTRONG X SIGNORA. This added to my interest, naturally. The flower was a rich salmon pink with a yellow base and quite fragrant. The foliage was leathery and glossy on a quite vigorous plant. Unhappily I was unable to get enough plants budded to supply the one hundred plants required for the AARS Test Gardens. In desperation I planted some DR. HUEY understock plants in five-gallon containers and put them under glass with the idea of budding enough plants to fill out our shortfall - about twenty plants. I did this but the plants looked so different from the field grown ones that I labeled each such plant "grown in a pot." This strategy avoided questions.

The Grandiflora I saved for entry did not present me with any problem as I was able to get enough plants budded in the field to supply the AARS Entry requirements. It was from a cross of ROUNDELAY X CRIMSON GLORY and was a truly remarkable color. It is described in Modern Roses as "dark orange red" and so it was. However, it was a good bit more than that as I saw it. The flower had a novel metallic quality, almost glittery, that so startled me when I first saw it that inadvertently the exclamation "Hell's Bells" slipped out. [This name was suggested for registration but frowned on by Beany Hutton (Sidney Jr.)-of all people.] The form of the flower was good as was the substance and there was no blue, at least in our climate. Unfortunately, the plant bristled with large prickles, was quite spreading in habit and could have used more vigor. The people at Conard-Pyle suggested the name WAR DANCE. Our agreement carried the right to both suggest names and to disapprove but not to finally approve. We all felt that was the natural and proper purview of the agency who had the responsibility of selling the plants. Ollie and I felt a good name was chosen and we let it go at that.

The Hybrid Tea scored in first place in its class in the AARS Trials but was voted down by the Trustees. It was regarded as lacking in novelty. The Conard-Pyle Co. introduced the variety and named it INVITATION. I have had many people tell me they grow it and like it. The failure to get an AARS Award after my special effort and my personal financial need was a blow. Even so Ollie was more disappointed than me - if that were possible. It is

75

suspected he felt he was being punished for helping me leave my former employment. After losing out on an AARS Award to FIRST LOVE, BUCCANEER, MANITOU and MONTEZUMA a few years before it was apparent to me that sometimes some of the Trustees were somewhat whimsical in their judgements. Sometimes they voted favorably at unexpected times!

As suggested earlier, Ollie Weeks, in his capacity as owner of Weeks Wholesale Rose Grower, gave us access to some varieties that Armstrong Nurseries did not grow. One of these was BABY CHATEAU which I used in several crosses but never got any noteworthy seedlings from my effort. I did discover that the flower buds were very dark and that the flowers had to be emasculated in quite tight bud to avoid self-pollination. When I observed the remarkable resemblance of the foliage to FLORA-DORA I began to do some speculating. It had been my observation that the climbing or rambling habit was dominant to the bush form of a rose plant. I had wondered how Mathius Tantau was able to get FLORADORA and its bush rose sisters by crossing BABY CHATEAU X ROSA ROXBURGHI. There seemed to be several things wrong with this position. First, if this cross were actually accomplished then the progeny should have all been climbers or ramblers as ROSA ROXBURGHI is definitely a rambler and we understand the rambling trait to be a dominant one. Although BABY CHATEAU has 28 chromosomes and would contribute fourteen of them to its offspring and ROSA ROXBURGHI could contribute only seven, the progeny from such a cross should still be rambling. Second, the offspring from such a cross should have been dominated by triploids with 21 chromosomes but FLORADORA, at least, had 28. FLORADORA has acted like a tetraploid (28 chromosomes) in crosses with other tetraploids and so has BABY CHATEAU. Thirdly, FLORADORA has no phenotypic resemblance to ROSA ROXBURGHI in plant or flower but does resemble BABY CHATEAU in flower color and even more in leaf and plant conformation. These factors coupled with our discovery that we must alter our normal procedure of emasculating BABY CHATEAU to avoid self pollination led us to the conclusion that, while Tantau no doubt thought he had produced FLORADORA from the cross he attempted, what actually happened was a self pollination of BABY CHATEAU. This should not detract from the importance of Tantau's achievement as all three of the supposed progeny of BABY CHATEAU X ROSA

ROXBURGHI made great contributions to the improvement in roses.

As indicated above, the variety ONDINE, a white was used in a cross with SUTTER'S GOLD at Armstrong Nurseries. ONDINE had a nicely formed flower and had the famous SOUVENIR DE CLAUDIUS PERNET as one parent. That cross was a disappointment as it produced nothing in either white or yellow Hybrid Tea type plant and flower. Armstrong introduced a seedling from the cross that was a Floribunda in habit and obtained a Prix di Roma Gold Medal with it. They named it MOONSPRITE. This seedling was such an unbelieveable result from the cross that was supposed to have produced it I feel confident an accidental mixture occurred in our seed or records at some point. I had only a mild interest in white roses. That degree of interest was appropriate as "mild" seems to describe the interest of the rose growing public. A rose listed by Roy Hennessey of Scappoose, Oregon under the name of VIRGO attracted our attention at Swim & Weeks, so we sent for a few plants. When I saw the flowers my interest became keen. It had beautiful long urn-shaped buds of pure white opening to flowers of good form with 25-30 petals. The flower substance was a bit soft and the plants were generously supplied with prickles, especially small ones. Ollie had been persuaded that I might as well carry on breeding for greenhouse cut-flower-type roses along with the garden rose project so I crossed PINOCCHIO X VIRGO. A white Sweetheart type, given the name WHITE CHARM, was one result and it had an almost immediate, although limited, acceptance in the florist trade by 1958. It would have had a longer life if it had not inherited so many small prickles from VIRGO.

At Armstrong Nurseries David Armstrong continued to observe and carry forward to introduction such of the seedlings left for his disposal as he and his father felt worthy. As I was obligated to assign plant patents on varieties they wished to introduce from the seedlings started in some way by me it was easy to keep track of them. In 1957 and 1958 assignments were made on GREEN FIRE from GOLDILOCKS X (FANDANGO X PINOCCHIO). The pollen parent here was probably CATHAY, which possibly was unnamed at the time of the name registration for GREEN FIRE. As might be deduced the Class was Floribunda, the flower greenish yellow - quite a striking color. HEAT WAVE was registered without giving the name of the seed parent. It was just listed Unnamed Seedling X ROUNDELAY, and classed a Flori-bunda, orange scarlet in color with about 26-36 petals. It was distinctive but not an outstanding rose. RUBY LIPS, another seedling from the cross of WORLD'S FAIR X PINOCCHIO, was described as "cardinal red" with 16 to 20 petals. This descriptive color term was one used often to indicate freedom from blue shades. RED GLORY, from GAY LADY X (PINOCCHIO X FLORADORA), was a curiosity - a bush that grew 8 to 10 feet in height where unrestricted. This reminded me that GAY LADY was only two generations removed from a Hybrid Rugosa. RED GLORY grows in my backyard to hide a chain link fence and provides a repeat riot of single bright red flowers. It mildews somewhat easily but a bit of diligence in spraying with Funginex takes care of that.

In November 1957 we experienced one of the most vicious Santa Ana winds in memory. Coming in the same year as our frozen seed flats might have seemed an omen if I were disposed to think along those lines. These winds are typically from northeast to southwest but this one was very nearly from east to west. Ollie owned a five-acre plot across the street from his home property, where our office and greenhouse were located. Swim & Weeks had leased this and I had planted all the seedlings produced from the 1955 and 1956 pollinations on it after providing some security by putting a chain link fence about it. I had also planted understock on this property and had reproduced our selected seedlings on that. The man farming the five acres just east of us had plowed, disced and harrowed in preparation for seeding to a crop for "green feed" for dairy cattle. When the winds began the soil began moving from our neighbor to our newest lot of seedlings then about a foot high. After three days of this I could only see the tips of some of the seedlings but then the wind ceased. I spent the next two weeks with a pick-up dump truck picking up the soil from around the seedlings with a square-point shovel and dumping it on a portion of the five acres then unplanted - a disheartening, exhausting experience. It seemed then that nothing went right that year but in retrospect it is clear that was not true. I was seeing some roses that were to be very important although I did not know then how important they were going to be.

In the meantime, David Armstrong was making selections from seedlings I had produced at Armstrong Nurseries and had reproduced by budding at least once before leaving. Previously I

78

referred to GARDEN PARTY that came along about this time. Others were distributed over a several year period near this time.   One of the more important, both for itself and for its role as a parent was EL CAPITAN, another seedling from the cross of CHARLOTTE ARMSTRONG X FLORADORA.   It was class-ed as a Grandiflora and described as having flowers "cherry to rose-red" in color with 25 to 35 petals.   It was a tremendously productive rose.   Three seedlings were released to other rose nurseries. CHERRY GLOW from a cross of FLORADORA X FIRST LOVE was a Grandiflora with medium size flowers of cherry red that had excellent substance and form.   It was introduced by C.R. Burr of Manchester, Connecticutt.   HIGH TIME from CHARLOTTE ARMSTRONG X SIGNORA and PINAFORE from CHINA DOLL X MRS. DUDLEY FULTON were both introduced by Roseway Nurseries of Beaverton, Oregon.   The former was a Hybrid Tea described as claret-rose with reverse gold and pink.   It had only 18 to 28 petals - its principal flaw.   PINAFORE had a mass of single dainty pink and yellow flowers on a small neat plant.   It is a cross made for a reason that now escapes me!

Chapter 9

AN ADDED PROJECT

In 1959 Swim & Weeks had another greenhouse cut-flower rose in JACK O'LANTERN from CIRCUS X GOLDEN SCEP-TER.   It was a multicolor and in the trade for about ten years.   It was one of the seedlings buried in sand after the 1957 sandstorm. Armstrong Nurseries introduced three more varieties left over from my effort.   One was COUNTY FAIR from a cross of FROLIC X PINK BOUNTIFUL.   It was what was often called a "Park Rose" at that time, having single medium pink flowers in great profusion - good for a mass color display.   DUET from FANDANGO X ROUNDELAY is a two-tone Hybrid Tea with inner surface of light pink and a reverse of dark pink to light red.   It was voted the Hybrid Tea AARS Winner for 1961.   PINK PARFAIT was the Winner of the AARS Award for 1961 in the Grandiflora Class.   It resulted when I crossed FIRST LOVE X PINOCCHIO.   It won not only that award but The Gold Medal of The National Rose Society and the Portland Gold Medal Certificate. It became a popular parent variety in Europe, especially in England.   After seeing it in Regent's Park in London it was easy to understand its popularity there.   A soft pink, it made the most effective bed in the Park but it was definitely a Floribunda there.   Another offspring worthy of note was EIFFEL TOWER from a cross of FIRST LOVE X (CHARLOTTE ARMSTRONG X SIGNORA).   That unnamed seedling was a light yellow with perhaps eighty relatively broad petals and quite fragrant.   It had a very large flower.   EIFFEL TOWER scored well in the AARS

Trials but did not win an Award because, as I remember, it was beaten by Bob Lindquist's GRANADA. It did win the Geneva (Switzerland) Gold Medal and the Rome Gold Medal (Prix di Roma). It was distinguished for its heavy fragrance, huge buds and tall growth. Armstrong Nurseries sold one other rose from my efforts that year. MERRY HEART was from EL CAPITAN X an unnamed seedling and was sold to C. R. Burr.

About 1960 Armstrong sold FIRST LADY, another of my seedlings, also to C. R. Burr. It resulted from FIRST LOVE X ROUNDELAY and was described as a Hybrid Tea of "rose madder to phlox-pink" with 18 to 22 petals. It was plain to see that I was enamored of both these parents, as they each were used in a variety of ways. It was about this time though that it became apparent that FIRST LOVE contributed to its offspring two qualities that needed to be offset by the other parent I mated with it. Its petals were a bit narrow and it did not give much to the size of the flowers of its offspring. FIRST LOVE had magnificent bud form and my early ambition was to have its bud form repeated in all colors. ROUNDELAY had the best substance and color combined with size of flower and production of anything I knew in this time. The Conard Pyle Co. put out INVITATION about 1961 - their second Swim & Weeks introduction. It was also about the time when Armstrong sold ALLURE to Interstate Nurseries of Hamburg, Iowa. It was the result of crossing MRS. PIERRE S. DUPONT X CHARLOTTE ARMSTRONG and was described as "Neyron Rose with yellow base." The next year my cross of CHARLOTTE ARMSTRONG X an unnamed seedling, which the Armstrongs decided to name JOHN S. ARMSTRONG after their founder, won the AARS Award for the Grandiflora Class. The "unnamed seedling" pollen parent was undoubtedly a derivative of FLORA-DORA. Also about this time, from my earlier effort, they introduced several roses that did very well in the AARS Trials but did not get Awards. These included SUMMER SUNSHINE from BUCCANEER X LEMON CHIFFON, a rich yellow that set a standard for flower bud form but which does not keep well as a cut flower and tends to burn on the plant in hot weather; COLUMBUS QUEEN from LA JOLLA X an unnamed seedling with two-tone pink flowers still appears in many a blue ribbon collection in rose shows. SIX FLAGS, another FIRST LOVE X ROUNDELAY Seedling was sold to Five M Nurseries of Tyler, Texas and to Poulsens of Denmark. It was described as cherry red in color.

Notable was its heritage of flower substance from its grandparent, FLORADORA. A seedling from the cross of CHARLOTTE ARMSTRONG X GIRONA drew my special attention because it was a yellow with 30 to 35 petals and was fragrant. The color was described as lemon-yellow to Indian yellow but neither the bud form nor flower form were very distinguished - some of the inner petals were petaloids rather than true petals and left the opening flower with a lack of character. It was sold to C. R. Burr who first named it CANADIANA but for some reason it was renamed IMPERIAL GOLD. It is assumed this was in response to encouragement from the American Rose Society. Had this seedling been available to me at Swim & Weeks it would surely have been used. The variety went through the AARS Trials but it is not remembered how it placed in the competition there. The plant had fair vigor, glossy, leathery leaves and its only flaw as a plant was a somewhat spreading habit. It had a much healthier look than SUMMER SUNSHINE or even SUTTER'S GOLD although not as vigorous as the latter. I would still explore the possibilities of this rose as a parent if I were still active.

Chapter 10

AARS AWARDS

About 1959, at least the year after INVITATION and WAR DANCE were entered in AARS Competition, Swim & Weeks made three entries in the Hybrid Tea Class and one entry in the Grandiflora Class.   One Hybrid Tea was a pink seedling from the cross of CHARLOTTE ARMSTRONG X SIGNORA, a fine rose in almost every way except that the color lacked novelty - an undistinguished pink.   Another entry was also from that cross but had orange-apricot petals with yellow edges - a distinctive color pattern and on a very vigorous plant well clothed with glossy, big leaves.   Its flaw was a stubby flower bud, lacking in the style I had set as my standard.   The third Hybrid Tea was from a cross of PEACE X VIRGO and was a lovely dainty pink that combined much of the best from its parents.   It had the big, dark green, glossy leaves of PEACE but with the upright habit and long flower buds of VIRGO and with more vigor than either variety.   The dainty coloring of the flower was exquisite - very pale pink center petals with deeper pink margins.   I had expected to get some whites but considered what I did get much preferable to white. When the first scores came in Ollie and I realized we were faced with a need for decision.   The undistinguished pink was in first place, the orange-apricot in second and the dainty pink in third.   I saw the first two as possibly presenting AARS with a problem, assuming the three roses maintained their position in the scoring through the next three scorings.   If the first two were rejected, and I assumed that possibility, past experience suggested the grave likelihood that the Trustees might very well reject the one in third place, just because it was in third place. Complicating the problem further was the fact that The Conard-Pyle Co. had options on all three varieties which they could exercise at any time before the completion of the Trials. My suggestion was that we withdraw the pink in first place and the orange-apricot in second place if we could obtain The Conard-Pyle Co.'s approval. Ollie, deferring to my previous experience, agreed to this. The decision makers at Conard-Pyle could understand our dilema and agreed to support our proposed action. We had been previously approached by Charlie Burr of C. R. Burr for a Hybrid Tea that his firm might introduce so we offered him the orange-apricot and he accepted, naming the variety HAWAIIAN SUNSET. That rose was immediately withdrawn from the Trials but it is not clear whether the deep pink was withdrawn then or whether it was left in and was outscored by the dainty pink or withdrawn just before the voting. In any event the dainty pink was voted on first and narrowly won an Award. Possibly we had the people at Conard-Pyle confused as they had not given us a decision on the option before the vote and by the terms of our agreement this stripped them of that privilege. However, after contemplating the added responsibilities the Award would add to Weeks Wholesale Rose Grower and its staff, Ollie decided to reinstate the option to Conard-Pyle. When The Conard-Pyle Co. had not taken up the option before the budding (propagation) season Ollie had budded a thousand understock in his fields the year before in preparation for sale of budwood to the prospective licenses the following summer. When Ollie re-offered the option to Conard-Pyle they accepted instantly on the condition that he supply all the budding eyes he could cut from his thousand plants. Ollie asked me to do this for him and the chore was gladly accepted. This yielded 20,000 budding eyes which were wrapped and stored in Ollie's walk-in refrigerator. The plants from which the budding eyes were cut were placed in a California cut-flower grower's greenhouses later and supplied additional budwood the following spring. John Lemon wrote us asking what we thought of the name "ROYAL HIGHNESS" for the rose. Everyone concerned approved and it was registered with The American Rose Society.

The Grandiflora rose we had entered in the same trials with ROYAL HIGHNESS was edged out by an entry from Jackson & Perkins Company which they had obtained from Mathias Tantau.

The latter had named it SUPER STAR for European distribution but Jackson & Perkins understandably did not want to distribute it in this country under that name as their competitor's (The Conard-Pyle Co.) trademark was "STAR ROSES." They received permission to use the commercial synonym TROPICANA. It was the great-grandchild of BABY CHATEAU! Our Grandiflora was a tall-growing white from a cross of QUEEN ELIZABETH X BLANCHE MALLERIN. It was not a very heavy bloomer and had rather small foliage inherited from "Blanche" but had a compensation in being exceptionally disease free. The Conard-Pyle people decided they would take up the option on it too. The name MOUNT SHASTA was registered with The American Rose Society.

David Armstrong was certainly diligent about screening and sifting over the seedlings left for him to evaluate. Eleven years after my departure Armstrong Nurseries were still releasing several from that collection each year. In 1963 names were registered for GRAND SLAM, a cherry to rose red Hybrid Tea from CHARLOTTE ARMSTRONG X MONTEZUMA and MATTER-HORN, a white Hybrid Tea from BUCCANEER X CHERRY GLOW, which won an AARS Award for 1966. This latter was an interesting genetic study. It should be remembered that CHERRY GLOW resulted from FLORADORA X FIRST LOVE and was cherry red in color. Normally I would not expect to cross a red rose to a yellow one and get a white. In this instance I did expect to as I had made a small cross of FLORADORA with a yellow previously and noted that I had strange color distribution among the resulting seedlings, some being white or nearly so. I expressed the suspicion then that the white color in some instances, and particularly in this one, was the result of some genic factor from FLORADORA acting as a color suppressant when in association with genes for yellow color causing white flowers to result.

In 1964 David registered BLITHE SPIRIT from FANDAN-GO X an unnamed seedling, a light pink Hybrid Tea of extreme vigor; JOSEPH'S COAT from BUCCANEER X CIRCUS was classified as a climber. This latter was a true novelty and well named. It had a profusion of semi-double flowers starting yellow and finishing red so that at any one time the colors ranged from yellow to pink to red. It won the Bagatelle Gold Medal. SWEET AFTON from (CHARLOTTE ARMSTRONG X

SIGNORA) X (ALICE STERN X ONDINE) was a pale blush Hybrid Tea, extremely fragrant and very vigorous. It was earlier remarked that nothing came from ONDINE and nothing did directly. This grandchild was the closest to achievement. In 1966 David cleaned up the last of the seedlings left with him. In that year he registered the name LUCKY LADY for my CHARLOTTE ARMSTRONG X CHERRY GLOW seedling that won an AARS Award in the Grandiflora Class. It was a two-toned pink which did not have much distinction but was very vigorous. Also in 1966 he registered the name LEMON SPICE for another of my seedlings - from HELEN TRAUBEL X an unnamed seedling, a very fragrant Hybrid Tea; and SEVENTH HEAVEN for still another from an unnamed seedling X CHRYSLER IMPERIAL - not a particularly distinctive red.

In this era Swim & Weeks released several Floribundas. The garden varieties were ones that Ollie decided to introduce through Weeks Wholesale Rose Grower. He and Verona, his wife, thought up names that would go with a "TALK" Series. The first of these was SWEET TALK a low growing bushy grower with lemon to white flowers that resulted when I crossed FROLIC X LAVENDER PINOCCHIO. Several others were given names in this series such as TOWN TALK from (CIRCUS X GARNETTE) X SPARTAN, a bright orange red; PLAIN TALK a non-bluing red from SPARTAN X GARNETTE. The reverse cross that produced SWEET TALK gave us a lavender Floribunda that we entered in the AARS Trials. It scored fairly well but appeared to have no chance to get an Award. As a consequence when Dave Stump, then Vice President of Armstrong Nurseries, asked us if it might be purchased we told him, "Yes", as the Conard-Pyle Co. had expressed no interest in it. Armstrong registered the name LILAC DAWN for it.

In 1963 we saw the culmination of the equivalent of a resurrection from the grave for four fine roses. A group of seedlings that survived the refrigeration freezing of 1956 and the sand burial of 1957 emerged to assume a variety of important roles. From them Swim & Weeks made a clean sweep of the roses voted AARS Awards for the introduction year of 1965. These were CAMELOT from a cross of CIRCUS X QUEEN ELIZABETH in the Grandiflora Class and MISTER LINCOLN from CHRYSLER IMPERIAL X CHARLES MALLERIN in the Hybrid Tea Class. Both these varieties were extremely vigorous, especially MISTER LINCOLN. On a visit to the AARS Garden at Armstrong Nurseries the plants of MISTER LINCOLN were found growing at ten feet. (David Armstrong's helpers had fertilized the garden rather heavily.) For some reason I did not notice the original plant of MISTER LINCOLN which was growing close to the end of a seedling row until it was about six feet tall. It had about fifty flowers on it in various stages of maturity and the thrill I experienced at that time is easily remembered. I resolved right then that it would be entered in the AARS Trials. A short time later I decided to try to get enough budding eyes off the original plant to make an entry. When I placed the buds in understocks there proved to be two hundred, an adequate number to make the entry. The previous year I had spotted an extremely dark red sister of this rose and had budded about fifteen plants, thinking to also bud enough for AARS Entry the following year if it still met with approval from both Ollie and me. As remembered Ollie somewhat favored the first one budded but I was utterly convinced that MISTER LINCOLN would outscore it in the AARS Trials. We both felt that both varieties were worthy of AARS Awards but were fully aware that the chances of such a thing happening were very small if they were competing against one another. I expressed the feeling that it would be better to waste a potential Award Winner in an effort to increase the chances of winning one Award rather than to take a chance on entering the two roses in separate years. As it turned out we did enter both varieties in the Spring of 1963. MISTER LINCOLN came in first and SWARTH-MORE, an entry of The Conard Pyle Co., was second and MISTER LINCOLN's sister came in third. Neither second nor third place got Awards. Ollie decided to introduce the very dark red through Weeks Wholesale Rose Grower and registered the name OKLAHOMA for it. It proved to be a big success on the market. Ollie's faith in it was not misplaced. Looking back now and remembering how well OKLAHOMA was received it seems possible that had OKLAHOMA been entered a year prior to MISTER LINCOLN we might have had an Award for each of them. That's greed for you!

Friends have asked me to explain in detail my reasons for making the cross that resulted in some of the more important seedlings. Such would of necessity include the cross of CHRYSLER IMPERIAL X CHARLES MALLERIN, the parents of MISTER LINCOLN and OKLAHOMA. At the time of

CHRYSLER IMPERIAL's introduction it represented the best red color we knew in Hybrid Tea varieties after CRIMSON GLORY. I do not remember seeing CHARLES MALLERIN before that nor do I remember it going through the AARS Trials. The introduction date of 1951 given for it in Modern Roses is also the year CHRYSLER IMPERIAL was voted an AARS Award. Be that as it may, when I saw CHARLES MALLERIN for the first time I saw qualities that were complementary to CHRYSLER IMPERIAL. Its dark red color appeared to have the same pigment quality I saw in WORLD'S FAIR - very dark but never burning in Ontario and free of blue. The flowers were as large as "Chrysler" but were not as well formed being flat without the high centers. Both varieties were vigorous and were widely separated in origin. Chrysler was more thickly branched and with superior plant habit but did not have as attractive leaves as "Mallerin". In other words I pictured an ideal composite that would carry lots of vigor, with flowers having the form of Chrysler, with the flower and leaf color of Mallerin, the plant habit of Chrysler and the reduced number of prickles characteristic of Mallerin. I did not quite attain such an ideal, as a rose breeder rarely does, but I did get two fine roses out of only 119 seedlings from that cross. Alain Meilland, Francis' son, told me he grew several thousand seedlings from this cross and selected only PAPA MEILLAND for introduction. I think PAPA MEILLAND represents a truer composite of the plant varieties but in our area it is not as big a flower or as vigorous a plant.

Two greenhouse cut-flower types were also survivors of both our disasters. I have mentioned JACK O'LANTERN earlier but not WHITE SATIN that resulted when I crossed MOUNT SHASTA X WHITE BUTTERFLY. WHITE SATIN, a Hybrid Tea, proved to be far more important than JACK O'LANTERN as it was widely grown both in the United States and Europe, especially in Holland where for some reason it was marketed under the name "WHITE WEEKEND". This rose marked an act in selection never tried before nor since by me. Both parent varieties had good form although WHITE BUTTERFLY had only been observed as a cut flower or growing under glass. All of the seedlings from the cross were planted in the field as there was no room in a greenhouse at the time they needed to be moved from the small peat pots. In looking at the flowers on the plants as they matured it was apparent that I was going to see nothing that would clearly have promise as a cut flower and that it would be necessary to do some interpolating. Reason told me that only a very double flower in the field would be likely to have enough petals to have any value under forcing conditions. As a consequence I selected a seedling with a flower that was extremely heavily petaled - even gross. Because of the good form of both parents it was not a total surprise when the seedling selected proved to have exquisite form under glass. The thrill of seeing it in our own greenhouse was not as great as when it was seen at a Roses, Incorporated convention exhibited by a cut-flower professional.

Armstrong Nurseries did not grow CHARLES MALLERIN but Weeks Wholesale Rose Grower did. The flower had a dark red color that in some unfathomable way suggested a color quality seen in such roses as WORLD'S FAIR, AMI QUINARD, LEMANIA, NIGHT and MIDNIGHT - very dark but generally resistant to burn in the climate at Ontario, California. CHARLES MALLERIN also had more substance (petal stiffness) than most of the "pure" Hybrid Tea kinds. Dr. Lammerts informed me he had grown a number of seedlings from the same cross without success. I was "triple blessed" to achieve two such roses as OKLAHOMA and MISTER LINCOLN from such a small population that survived two disasters. OKLAHOMA did not have as clear red as MISTER LINCOLN nor did it grow as tall but its flowers were larger and it had petals with greater substance. Both varieties were very fragrant, MISTER LINCOLN at its best in the morning when it is cool and OKLAHOMA at midday when it is warmer.

CAMELOT was a somewhat curious result from CIRCUS X QUEEN ELIZABETH. It was more vigorous than either parent and with larger leaves. It was very resistant to mildew but somewhat susceptible to Rose Rust. It was used some as a parent and again it was surprising. The flowers on the seedlings resulting from crosses with Hybrid Tea varieties were unusually large, even for Hybrid Teas. CAMELOT has an unusual color. The best we could describe it was "salmon" or "shrimp-pink". Its weakness was lack of flower form and consistency. At its best a truly lovely flower and with an unusual fragrance that was described as spicy. The bud form was ovoid - not long and urn-shaped.

In 1965 Swim & Weeks registered the name ORANGE GARNET for a greenhouse cut-flower "Sweetheart" resulting from a cross of (GARNETTE X CIRCUS) X SPARTAN. As the name suggests the color was orange red.   One day I was visiting the cut flower ranges of Armacost & Royston in Santa Monica to look at our seedlings on trial as prospective cut-flower varieties. While there the manager came out with a French nurseryman, whom I had not previously met.   His name was Paul Pekmez and he had asked to meet me as he had a flower of ORANGE GARNET in his lapel and wanted an opportunity to test it and perhaps distribute it in Europe.   The manager at Armacost vouched for Pekmez so he was told I would send him some budding eyes.   This led to a more involved relationship and I was soon sending him more varieties for test.   The most successful were ORANGE GARNET and WHITE SATIN.   In 1966 we had two more greenhouse cut-flower Floribundas put on the market for us by Carlton Rose Nurseries of Carlton, Oregon.   They were GOLDEN SHEEN from OPHELIA X CIRCUS and PINK FLAIR from VERONA X ESCORT.   Their names describe their color.   The mention of VERONA reminds us that this beautiful Sweetheart was produced in 1963 and was for some time our best cut-flower variety in this class.   It was named in honor of Verona Weeks, of course.   It was produced as a result of a selection from the cross of SPARTAN X GARNETTE.

At some point a cross of WORLD'S FAIR X CHRYSLER IMPERIAL was made and the result was an unusual product.   Just where this one seedling fit in classification I did not know.   The plant was larger than CHRYSLER IMPERIAL and much bushier. The leaves were very mildew resistant, medium to large, flat, medium green, non-glossy and clothed the plant copiously.   The flower was intermediate in size between the two parents and never turned blue at any stage.   The shape of the bud was ovoid and the flower opened flat with about 25 to 30 petals.   It had no clusters at any time that we observed so it seemed to fit neither Floribunda nor Grandiflora.   The flowers were somewhat small for the size of the plant so was not an impressive Hybrid Tea.   However, this seedling combined health of plant and foliage, color purity, and vigor so that I used it in several crosses.   In one instance it was used as a seed parent in a cross to HAPPINESS.   One result was a garden rose put out by Weeks Wholesale Rose Grower under the registered name of NIGHT 'N' DAY.   It was a Hybrid Tea with tall habit, long stems and long flower buds.   The substance of the flowers was exceptionally good but the color was too dark for acceptance by the florists even though some tried it for a few years.   The dark color was reminiscent of CHARLES MALLERIN but the plant was shaped totally different - more like HAPPINESS but without the big prickles.   NIGHT 'N' DAY was very upright and neat in habit whereas CHARLES MALLERIN was spreading-awkward and not as floriferous as NIGHT 'N' DAY.

A personal ambition was to breed and select a red Hybrid Tea that would dominate the cut-flower market as a variety bred by Robert Jelly of E. G. Hill Company of Richmond, Indiana was doing in the middle sixties.   The name registered for the Jelly variety was FOREVER YOURS.   Its parentage was listed as YULETIDE X unnamed seedling.   It was described as "cardinal-red" but there was considerable blue in its makeup.   By the time it had been in the florist's refrigerator for a day or two it often had a strong purple cast.   E. G. Hill Company had for a couple of generations led the florist industry in breeding and marketing cut roses.   John Lemon, related to E. G. Hill, continued to encourage my goal as long as he was alive.   It was John's conviction that the best winter producing Hybrid Tea varieties were descended from OPHELIA.   This rose, in truth, was related in some fashion to several generations of early Hybrid Teas that were offered to the florist trade as "red".   I speculated as to why this might be.   The parentage of OPHELIA was not known or was deliberately concealed.   It was among the early Hybrid Teas though over forty years after the introduction of LA FRANCE, generally credited with being the first one.   I used OPHELIA only once, successfully, in producing GOLDEN SHEEN when it was crossed to CIRCUS.   About all this showed me was that I had reason to believe that OPHELIA may have been a chance offspring of a yellow rose as I had suspected.   Another conclusion was that the Tea Rose strain was responsible for the continuous bloom cycles.   I was reminded that nearly all the climbing sports of modern garden roses bloomed principally in the spring and often not again during a calendar year.   This did not apply to CLIMBING TALISMAN which normally bloomed heavily in the autumn as well as in the spring.   It often had scattered flowers in between these heavier blooms.   TALISMAN (the bush) was stated to be from the cross of OPHELIA X SOUVENIR DE CLAUDIUS PERNET and was bred by Montgomery, a green-house cut-flower grower and breeder of roses.   TALISMAN was an extremely popular cut-flower rose for about twenty years as it was both a novelty and had good production during the winter months when the market demand was at its peak.   At Swim &

93

Weeks I attempted to use TALISMAN but found nothing of value in the seedlings from it - not because the plants would not bloom in the winter but because I could not combine that quality with a bloom color and shape that would be desired in the market.

After my generally unsatisfactory results from using OPHELIA and its relatives my attention was attracted to PINOCCHIO inasmuch as Gene Bourner had used it so successfully in breeding cut-flower Floribunda kinds. My most successful cut-flower rose thus far was VERONA from SPARTAN X GARNETTE. A sister of VERONA, PLAIN TALK was a good shade of red and larger flowered than most of the progeny from the cross. I decided to cross NIGHT 'N' DAY to PLAIN TALK. A seedling resulted that interested me and the range superintendent at Armacost & Royston in 1966. "B-4" had the color and production qualities we wanted but not the shape. To my regret this appeared about the time of my retirement and was not much used in subsequent crosses.

Chapter 11

NEW GOALS

Two roses grown by Weeks Wholesale Rose Grower that were not grown by Armstrong Nurseries and that were felt worthy of study were LAVENDER PINOCCHIO and STERLING SILVER. LAVENDER PINOCCHIO was unique for the range of color produced in the flowers during their progress from opening to maturity. As they opened the blooms had a distinctly brownish cast but by the time the flowers were fully open they had become lavender. The variety had been introduced by Jackson & Perkins and was the product of Eugene Boerner who obtained it by crossing PINOCCHIO X GREY PEARL. (GREY PEARL is generally thought to be the first introduction in the lavender color range. It was a McGredy production which that firm called THE MOUSE. J & P had obtained the USA introduction rights and renamed it GREY PEARL.) STERLING SILVER was bred by Gladys Fisher who was associated with a prominent cut-flower grower of roses but she turned it over to the Jackson & Perkins Company for distribution to the garden trade. At the time of its release it was the closest thing to a blue rose on the market. I am confident it would have been far more widely distributed if it had been more vigorous. Its color was actually a pale lavender. When grown under the protection of a greenhouse it did have a silvery color.

I made several different crosses involving LAVENDER PINOCCHIO. They were exploratory in nature. At the time I was unable to identify the source of the lavender color. The McGredy roses shown as involved in GREY PEARL were mostly reds with the exception of MRS. CHARLES LAMPLOUGH and FRAU KARL DRUSCHKI which were pale yellow and white respectively. There is some confusion and shortage of information as is the case with many older roses but there does seem to be some heritage from ROSA FOETIDA BICOLOR (AUSTRIAN COPPER). Mr. E. B. LeGrice of Roseland Nurseries, Norfolk, England had written somewhere of his conviction that the expression of lavender color in roses occurs only when factors for yellow pigment are present. Somewhere we got the impression that the pigments causing the expression of ivory color were also important. Remembered are crosses of LAVENDER PINOCCHIO X FROLIC and CIRCUS X LAVENDER PINOCCHIO at an early stage of the new partnership. One result was LILAC DAWN from the former cross, mentioned earlier as having been sold to Armstrong Nurseries. A white Floribunda resulted from the reciprocal of that cross and was named SWEET TALK, introduced by Weeks Wholesale Rose Grower.

Nothing was introduced directly from the cross of CIRCUS X LAVENDER PINOCCHIO but one Floribunda from that cross with lavender colored flowers and a very healthy, vigorous plant was selected to cross to STERLING SILVER. In this combination I felt assured of a lavender colored flower. It seemed I should have a good chance for more petals than STERLING SILVER and could expect some contribution from that variety towards bud and flower form. It was hoped the unnamed seedling would contribute plant vigor. I was fortunate in not being disappointed with respect to any of these features. A seedling was selected from the resulting population and multiplied for entry in the 1965 AARS Trials. It had an unusual reddish overlay of color in the opening flower that changed to deep lavender as the blooms became fully open. This I attributed to its heritage from CIRCUS. To add to the novelty the blooms contained about thirty petals arranged mostly in perfect symmetry. The flowers had a unique and strong fragrance that we likened to anise. This variety won an AARS Award for 1969 introduction. The Conard-Pyle Co. introduced it, made one of the best color plates ever seen and named the variety ANGEL FACE.

Gene Boerner of Jackson & Perkins had used his rose SPARTAN to produce a number of interesting Floribunda roses and I had used it in producing some "Sweetheart" roses for the cut-flower florist trade. These had been so good that I resolved to

96

explore the use of SPARTAN in crosses with Hybrid Teas.   I felt this rose might have special value in seeking non-bluing reds with the ability to continue bloom through the winter.   I had earlier made a cross of CARROUSEL X HAPPINESS with the intent of getting a garden red with more production out-of-doors than experienced with HAPPINESS.   At the time we had no thought about a cut-flower rose.   HAPPINESS, a production of Francis Meilland with rather involved parentage, was grown some for the garden but was the best quality red Hybrid Tea rose for greenhouse cut-flower use.   Its principal flaw for that market was low productivity, particularly in the winter months, a trait that was of little concern in the garden.   Just what kind of rose I got from the CARROUSEL cross is not remembered - presumably some degree of intermediacy.   CARROUSEL had flowers of good red color quality but not distinguished for form.   It was classed as a Grandiflora - tall and with some degree of clustering.   At any rate I found a seedling from the cross I felt inspired to cross to SPARTAN.   One of the resulting seedlings had a fine combination of deep orange-red color, fine substance and form of flower.   We entered this selection in AARS Competition and won an Award in the Grandiflora Class for introduction in the class of 1969 - with ANGEL FACE.   Both roses were introduced by The Conard-Pyle Co., who named the Grandiflora COMMANCHE.   It needs moderately warm weather to produce its best color which is a deep orange-red.   The petals have good substance.

The year before, Swim & Weeks had entered a white Hybrid Tea in the AARS Trials that scored very well but did not get enough votes for an Award.   Ollie decided to put the variety out under the name of PALOMA.   It was the result of crossing MOUNT SHASTA X WHITE KNIGHT, making it a half-sister to the greenhouse rose, WHITE SATIN.   It is frequently seen in local gardens.   Its fine substance and flower form, together with its healthy big leaves and strong growth, make it one of my favorite white Hybrid Teas in today's gardens.

Chapter 12

SEMI-RETIREMENT

In 1967 an accumulation of health problems made it seem wise for me to think of retirement. Ollie Weeks was advised of my desire to dissolve the partnership and negotiations began in August of that year and were concluded by the following December. David Armstrong was leaving his job as Research Director at Armstrong Nurseries to begin studies at the medical school of Creighton University and I was asked to take over his office duties and the making of the crosses in the Research Department while searching for a replacement for David. This latter job took two or three years as I found few people trained for this specialized job who were available. The Jackson & Perkins Company had lost both Gene Boerner and Charlie Perkins by death during this period. The J & P Company had for a number of years split their Research Department, with a New York installation and another in Northern California in the general area of Pleasanton. Charlie Perkins, as President, had hired Dr. Dennison Morey as his on-site rose breeder for the California operation. "Denny", as he was called, was "Charlie's man" and did not have to answer to Gene. Gene was expected to aid Charlie in selecting promising seedlings in the California operation. They did this periodically by flying out together and looking over the many thousands of seedlings while riding down the rows on a tractor, each over one row. Denny was also expected to make seedling selections since naturally many seedlings bloomed at times when Charlie and Gene were not present. I was told that Denny produced each year as many as

100,000 seedlings at Pleasanton. Presumably, Denny intended to exhaust the combination possibilities with this technique. In theory this might seem a sound approach. In practice I question any individual's or group of individuals' ability to productively analyze the content of such huge populations. It seems to me that a very large percentage would have flowers that went unobserved and unevaluated. I never tried to produce more than ten or twelve thousand seedlings per year and yet I am convinced even at that level many seedlings escaped my attention.

About the time of Charlie Perkins' death Denny left the firm and William Warriner was hired to take his place. "Bill" became responsible for the New York operation after Gene Boerner's death. It occurred to me that Gene must have had an assistant who had been passed over. Inquiry disclosed this to be correct and that the man's name was Arnold Ellis. One of the men on the office staff at Armstrong had been previously employed by J & P, knew Arnold Ellis and gave us his concept of a character sketch. This led to my contacting Arnold and setting up an interview in Rochester. This was followed by a visit from him and his wife, Julie, to Armstrong Nurseries in Ontario. After an interview by John Armstrong, Arnold was offered a job and decided to accept it. After about a year on the job Arnold (who had become "Arnie" by this time) and the Personnel Director hired an assistant for him by the name of Jack Christensen. My time had been shortened to three days a week and at my suggestion Arnie became Director of Research. One of the job attractions for Arnie was that during his training period he would be qualified as co-inventor of the seedlings on which we applied for plant patent. A part of his duties would be to look at seedlings with me and by himself. The actual pollinations were made by a Fred Carlson and his helper, Bobbie Boyd (a girl), who worked from a list made for them by me. Fred and Bobbie took care of the maintenance and planting as well.

Chapter 13

A GLIMPSE OF ROSE EUROPE

One of the inducements John Armstrong, Jr. had held out to me, when the job was offered, was a trip to Europe to visit the various agents the company had there. This included agents for fruit trees as well as for roses. I had made contact with many of these by letter before leaving Armstrong Nurseries in 1954 and had also arranged for some of them to distribute Swim & Weeks roses after Ollie and I had some new varieties available. Part of my job on the trip was to offer distribution to leading rose breeders whom I felt might not have exclusive arrangements for U.S. distribution. Armstrong Nurseries already had introduced new roses from Louis Lens of Belguim, Jean Gaujard and Georges Delbard of France, R. Harkness and Company of England, and Poulsen of Denmark. Kordes had introduced many Armstrong roses in Germany, Rolf Buisman in Holland. Sam McGredy IV had tested Armstrong seedlings in Northern Ireland.

The first World Rose Conference was held in London in early July 1968. I had been asked to be on the program and had accepted with John Armstrong's approval. Helen, my wife, who was to go with me, quit her job of ten years as school secretary at Vernon Junior High School in Montclair. John suggested we put some pleasure breaks in our itinerary and this proved to be wise from our view as seven weeks is a long time to live out of a suitcase. Our schedule called for us to attend an AARS Press Conference in New York before flying to Amsterdam where we were to be met by Conrad Hartgerinck, the retired range superintendent at Armacost & Royston. He was a native of Holland and was visiting there. Conrad had volunteered to be our transportation, interpreter and guide while we were in Holland and proved to be a jewel in his new Mercedes. Two days were spent at the establishment and in the company of G. Verbeek of Aalsmeer who was the Dutch distributor of some of Swim & Weeks greenhouse cut-flower roses - particularly WHITE SATIN. Mr. Verbeek, the breeder of DR. A.J. VERHAGE (GOLDEN WAVE), and Conrad took us to visit the famous flower market at Aalsmeer where many acres all under one roof are devoted to the sale of various types of horticultural products, including cut flowers of roses and carnations.

Our next stop was Rome where we were met by Dr. Anseloni, agent for various protected Armstrong products, principally peach and nectarine varieties. We did not see many roses here but Anseloni took us by the garden where the roses in competition for the Prize of Rome (Prix di Roma) were growing. It was too early to see much.

From Rome our itinerary took us next to Nice, France, from which focal point we visited the Meilland establishment at Cap d'Antibe where their rose breeding took place - all under glass. Our timing was not good as the funeral of a member of the family had occurred the same day we arrived. Alain had no opportunity to inform us so we visited with Helene, Alain's first wife, who was partially confined to bed at that time. The next day Alain drove us to St. Andre, some miles inland, where the Meilland growing grounds were located. Alain had propagated a surprising number of seedlings in some quantity. His father, Francis, who died in 1957, had formed an inter-European rose organization inspired by All-America Rose Selections but designed somewhat differently in order to provide a cooperative agency for the distribution of new Meilland roses. Francis had also formed an organization with the acronym of CIOPORA, the full name of which was in French. The actual words are no longer remembered but Armstrong Nurseries became a member at my recommendation. Francis Meilland was not a lawyer but had studied the French Law on patents and concluded it would provide protection for new plants. He subsequently applied for protection on one of his new roses and personally prosecuted his case before a French tribunal to a successful conclusion. He was a brilliant man and an inspired rose breeder.

Alain helped put us on a train to Marseilles where we transferred to a train that took us to Nimes, France, the location of Lambertin Nurseries. Aime Lambertin spoke English with a British accent having learned it by listening to broadcasts of the British Broadcasting Company over his radio. He had visited the Armstrong Nurseries in Ontario to observe the peach and nectarine varieties produced in the Research Department. Lambertin Nurseries did not grow nor sell roses and neither did Juan Orero of Segorbe, Spain, the next stop on our tour. We stayed in Valencia while visiting Orero as the accommodations were better.

From Valencia our next stop was London and the First World Rose Conference. This provided an opportunity to meet rose breeders and growers from many of the countries of the world where roses were grown. Many such were on the program like myself. This included Sam McGredy IV and Pat Dickson of Northern Ireland; Jack Harkness, Harry Wheatcroft, E. B. LeGrice and John Mattock, all of England; Alec Cocker of Scotland; Niels Poulsen of Denmark; Reimer Kordes of Germany; Herman Buss of South Africa; and Mr. and Mrs. (Doug and Esme) Butcher of New Zealand. Many of our friends from the United States were there too.

Our arrival coincided with Wimbledon. We did not go, but we were able to watch some of it on television from our room in the hotel. We were staying in the London Hilton and the evening before the finals we spotted Arthur Ashe in the lobby of our hotel. He was slated to play Rod Laver in the final of the men's singles on the following day. On impulse I walked up to him, told him I was from Southern California and wished him luck. He thanked me and said "I'll need it." He was correct as Rod Laver was at the top of his game and beat Arthur pretty soundly.

After my obligation to the program was discharged we had the opportunity to take a bus out to St. Albans where the Royal National Rose Society conducts trials for roses from all over the world. This is also headquarters for The Society. The beds are laid out in beautiful fashion and provide a very satisfactory landscape effect. Just how much space they occupy is not known but probably not more than two or three acres with the head-quarters building.

One morning the visitors and guests of the Conference were invited to visit Regent's Park, a magnificent garden, perhaps a half

103

mile long and about fifty yards wide. This is devoted mostly to roses but there are many beds of other flowers too. Many of the roses were at their peak of bloom. As mentioned earlier, a bed of PINK PARFAIT was one of the most impressive. After seeing it there it was more easily understood how it had won the Royal National Rose Society Gold Medal and why Jack Harkness has used it in his breeding program. It was not a Grandiflora there -just a typical Floribunda.

The Queen Mother gave a reception for the attendees of the Rose Conference from abroad. It was given in St. James Palace where there is no air conditioning and the weather outside was close to 100° F. Helen and I attended and can attest that it must have been equally hot in St. James Palace. We felt it remarkable that the Queen Mother showed no evidence of distress. A very gracious lady she was.

From London we flew to Strasbourg, France on the Rhine River. This was to visit Paul Pekmez, the proprietor of NIRP, a grower and distributor of roses throughout Europe through his agents in the various countries. I found it interesting to observe seedling roses of my origination in Paul's nursery rows and to have his critical comments. I remember discovering that Paul did not care for roses of really good vigor with such height that he could not look down on the flowers. This reminded me of impressions of many years before to the effect that European breeders were so concerned with novelty that their product often did not have enough vigor to give satisfaction in gardens in many parts of America.

Pekmez had a chalet in The Voges (French equivalent of The Black Forest of Germany) to which he took us. When we arrived we were met by two little orphan boys whom Paul and Marlyse, his wife, had adopted. Also waiting for us were a natural son, Pierre, a boy of seventeen and a daughter, Genevieve, who was about twenty-one. Genevieve was interested in learning how to make crosses of roses. Through a cousin, who could interpret, I was able to show her the mechanics of rose breeding and she was delighted. Paul kept a horse or two at this mountain hideaway and the previous summer had built a steeple-chase race track, not far from the chalet. He told us that he had moved 100,000 cubic meters of soil in building the track. Obviously Paul loved horses and racing. He did not forget roses in building that track, however. He had planted Floribunda roses around the entire

104

circumference of the track. Asked if there were purses for the winning owners, Paul said, "No, just a bunch of friends bring their horses to race." One got the impression there might be some heavy side bets. Our next stop was to be Hamburg, Germany from where we had dates to meet Mathias Tantau in Uetersen and Reimer Kordes in Sparrieshoop on succesive days. On learning we were taking the train from Strasbourg, Marlyse urged us to stop off at Stuttgart to see Killesberg Gardens and the festival that occurred every Saturday during the summer. We did and were very glad we did. Killesberg Gardens is a florist's dream. A very large part of the Park (for that is what it is) is devoted to beds of various kinds of flowers. Fresh flowers are brought out of greenhouses as the old ones pass maturity so all the Park is a riot of fresh flowers all summer. At the end of the day we noticed an increasing number of children coming in. We also became aware that jack o'lanterns in various patterns were distributed around the grounds and in the shrubbery. At dusk some sort of explosive signal sounded and the children ran to the jack o'lanterns with lighted punks in hand and soon had all the candles lighted. As it grew dark the Park became a fairyland.

I had written both Mathias Tantau and Reimer Kordes setting up our times for meeting. Mr. Tantau had been invited to lunch but pleaded a prior engagement. Reimer Kordes agreed to have lunch with us on the following day. After arriving in London we had made the acquaintance of Herman Buss of South Africa whom Sam McGredy had recommended. On comparing notes it was discovered Mr. Buss was going to be in Hamburg the same time we were. He invited us to have lunch with him and since we were not lunching with Mr. Tantau we agreed to meet him after seeing Tantau.

On going to Uetersen we were not met immediately by Mr. Tantau but by his foreman, Hans Evers, who began showing us about through the greenhouses on the grounds with the Tantau residence. After a little time Mr. Tantau joined us and continued with us throughout the rest of the morning. At noon he surprised me by asking if Helen and I could have lunch with Mrs. Tantau and himself. On being told that we had made other plans he seemed disappointed - so seemingly we had not understood one another. We did meet Herman Buss and had a very enjoyable lunch followed by a cruise on the Elbe River. The two most memorable roses at Tantau's were FRAGRANT CLOUD and WHISKEY MAC. The name for FRAGRANT CLOUD in Germany was DUFTWOLKE.

At W. Kordes' Sohne the following day we were met by Reimer and had a fascinating but somewhat discouraging experience. We saw seedlings that made me feel envious - beautiful forms and colors. They were principally Floribundas, however. We asked Reimer if his firm was able to send Armstrong Nurseries any Hybrid Tea seedlings for test and possible introduction. I knew his firm had introduced varieties through Jackson & Perkins but did not know if their agreement with that firm was an exclusive one. He agreed to see what could be done. We had lunch together and went back to our hotel in Hamburg. From there we were originally scheduled to fly to Copenhagen but discovered at the last minute that Niels Poulsen, whom we were to see there, was in Northern Ireland at Sam McGredy's and was slated to be on the same show jury on which I had agreed to serve. We canceled our flight to Copenhagen and took a flight to Belfast, Northern Ireland instead.

Chapter 14

NORTHERN IRELAND

Sam McGredy and I had been friends since his first visit to Armstrong Nurseries in 1948. (He claims he was only interested in Hollywood and the starlets at that time. I think he was nineteen then!) By 1968, when we were ready to go to Europe, we had received many visits from Sam. As soon as he knew we were coming to Northern Ireland he had arranged for me to be a part of the jury that would judge the new roses in the international competition held in Lord and Lady Dixon Park near Belfast. Our hotel was in downtown Belfast, right next to the railroad station that was to be the target of Irish terrorists the next year. We had barely settled into our room when we had a call from the wife of Sam's manager. She informed us that we were to be Sam's guests at a dinner in a pub on the shore of Lough Neigh where she and her husband would drive us. This proved to be an international gathering as Niels Poulsen, Hete Spek (son of Jan Spek of Holland) and several other Europeans were present but Helen and I were the only Americans. The main course was fried eel caught in Lough Neigh. Helen had some misgivings but found this not bad fare at all. I enjoyed it much more than many varieties of fish that I had eaten. The entertainment, aside from the conversation, was provided by a children's dance class performing native Irish folk dances.

Part of the time during our stay in Northern Ireland Helen and I were guests of Sam at his then new home in Portadown, adjacent to his nursery. Sam invited me to view his new seedling selections and I was privileged to see some of his first "hand-painted" series. These were spectacular. Subsequently Armstrong Nurseries were privileged to introduce his first release of that group of seedlings - one he named PICASSO. Sam lists it as a seedling from MARLENA X [EVELYN FISON X (FRUHLINGSMORGEN X ORANGE SWEETHEART)]. In Northern Ireland, where I first saw it, this rose had a flower three inches in diameter with a white eye and a red band of about one-quarter inch at the outer edge of each petal. It had about fifteen petals. Unfortunately, at Ontario, California this rose only occasionally displayed the white eye. The plant was neat, however, and the orange-red color was totally unblemished by blue. Of this group of roses we think a later release named MATANGI was more spectacular than PICASSO. Sam showed its parentage as an Unnamed Seedling X PICASSO. It had a larger flower and the banding was more spectacular. A rose breeder is always thrilled when a new "break" is achieved by any breeder. The greatest thrill, naturally, comes when such is one's own. It is special too when a friend like Sam McGredy gets one -with a family tradition to live up to.

Helen and I spent a full week in Northern Ireland with one day devoted to family research. My maternal grandmother was born in County Tyrone, adjacent to County Armagh where Sam's home and nursery were located at that time. Not wanting to test my driving skill in a country where one drives on the left we hired a driver from the Tourist Bureau. That proved fortunate as our driver led us to sources we could not possibly have found without his help. In addition he drove us to Enniskillen on Lough Erne in County Fermanagh on the west coast. We found a record of great-grandfather's death and an aunt and uncles' birth in Augher. We also spent a fun day without strain.

At some point during our week in Northern Ireland we visited Hawlmark, the nursery and breeding station of the Dickson family. This establishment is located at Newtownards in County Down on the east coast, about ten miles straight east of Belfast at the north end of Strangford Lough (lake). In the morning of our visit Pat Dickson, the fifth generation of rose breeder in the Dickson Family, took me on a tour of their rose nursery where I saw many varieties not then in America. Some that were in America were remembered as inferior to what was being seen at Dickson's of Hawlmark. The climate there is much kinder than the dry, hot environment of Ontario, California. REDGOLD, Pat's seedling, at that time a fairly recently AARS Award was especially fine and comparable to what we had seen in Oregon and Washington. Pat arranged for a driver to take us to an estate of the Londonderry Family that had been donated to public use. As remembered the location was on an isthmus between Strangford Lough and the Irish Sea. It was being maintained as a botanic garden and while it was not funded sufficiently to be well kept it did have much of interest for one deeply interested in plants. It seemed amazing that plant varieties too cold-tender to be grown in Southern California managed to survive in that location - about the same latitude as Vancouver, British Columbia! Such plants as the more tender species of flowering Eucalyptus and Bouganvillea seemed to be out of place. The mysterious influence of water currents from Strangford Lough must have contributed some warmth. That day ended with a delightful dinner at the Pat Dickson home where we met Anisley, Pat's gracious wife, and their two children.

Chapter 15

LEFT OVERS

At the time of my leaving Swim & Weeks there were two roses in the All-American Competition that did not get Awards but were introduced by Weeks Wholesale Rose Grower. BIENVENU, a Grandiflora, was a rose from the cross of CAMELOT X (MONTEZUMA X WAR DANCE). A bright reddish-orange of abundant and fragrant bloom. This rose had many flowers of magnificent form but many of the side blooms in the clusters tended to be too heavy for their stems, especially when rained on or watered overhead. SONRISA, a Hybrid Tea, was from a cross of MISTER LINCOLN X NIGHT 'N' DAY. It was a disappointment. We had hoped to recover the color of CHARLES MALLERIN and at the same time keep the plant habit of either of the direct parents. We got the latter but not the former. SONRISA had very fragrant flowers and the plant was very vigorous but the color was a purplish red - not what I had hoped for at all.

In the 1970 Introduction year a seedling of Gene Boerner's won the only AARS Award. FIRST PRIZE was introduced after his death. In my eyes it was the finest thing he ever did - comparable to PEACE. In it Gene achieved the bud form of FIRST LOVE without that varieties' narrow petals. It proved to be an exhibitor's delight and won many a "Queen of Show." The registration showed it to have resulted from a cross of ENCHANT-MENT Seedling X GOLDEN MASTERPIECE Seedling. We were impressed enough with the form and substance of FIRST PRIZE's flowers that we used it substantially as a parent following its introduction.

Before leaving Armstrongs for med-school David Armstrong had entered a Grandiflora in the AARS Trials that subsequently won an AARS Award for the Introduction Year of 1971. It was named AQUARIUS. Its origin is of interest - a seedling resulting from a somewhat involved background - (CHARLOTTE ARMSTRONG X CONTRAST) X [FANDANGO X (WORLD'S FAIR X FLORADORA)]. The crosses "sound" familiar but I do not know specifically what the seedlings were. David had also budded seedlings of his origination for entry in the following year and had asked me as a special favor to not set them aside - in other words not to change direction. This seemed only fair and I carried out his wishes. One of his seedlings won an AARS Award as a Hybrid Tea for the Introduction year 1972. It was named APOLLO and resulted from a cross that I too would have expected to result in good things. It was HIGH TIME X IMPERIAL GOLD. HIGH TIME in turn came from CHARLOTTE ARMSTRONG X SIGNORA. It was lacking in petalage and had been sold to Roseway Nurseries because of that. IMPERIAL GOLD was from a cross of CHARLOTTE ARMSTRONG X GIRONA. IMPERIAL GOLD came close to being the rose of a dream. The yellow color was rich, the size of the flower was average, the foliage was dark and glossy, the plant was upright and vigorous. The only quality that kept it from being a rose of distinction was its lack of form. The petals were on the whole a bit narrow, deteriorating to petaloids in the center, sometimes with red streaks on the latter. Understandably APOLLO had some of the same shortcomings as its parents and probably won an AARS Award primarily because of its vigor. It is ironic that David Armstrong won AARS Awards on two roses that lacked something in distinction and got no competitive awards for three roses that are recognized by many as outstanding. These three are OLE, a Grandiflora, from the cross of ROUNDELAY X EL CAPITAN; SAN ANTONIO another Grandiflora from the same cross; and CENTURY TWO, a Hybrid Tea resulting from a cross of CHARLOTTE ARMSTRONG X DUET. OLE unfortunately was in the same competition as our CAMELOT and was not as vigorous but we think it is a better rose. It has adequate vigor, the foliage is dense and glossy, the color of the flowers is a gorgeous dark orange-red with plenty of petals and fine form. SAN ANTONIO when grown to its best performance can be of exhibition quality but in the average garden is a prolific producer of good red colored flowers with about thirty five petals and with mildew resistant foliage. It narrowly missed being useful as a greenhouse cut-flower when it did not have quite the petal substance required. CENTURY TWO was referred to by some as an "Improved CHARLOTTE ARMSTRONG". It had flowers and plant that resembled that parent except "more so". The plant was more vigorous than its mother and the flowers had broader petals and a bit softer color. CENTURY TWO like OLE had the misfortune of competing against PORTRAIT in the Hybrid Tea Class and being barely outscored by that variety. We believe PORTRAIT was the first AARS Winner to be bred by an amateur. Carl Meyer got PORTRAIT by crossing PINK PARFAIT X PINK PEACE. It is technically a good rose but we do not see it a blue ribbon winner in rose shows as often as CENTURY TWO.

Back at Armstrong Nurseries the breeding of cut-flower roses for the greenhouse and florist trade was picked up again. GOLDSTRIKE was crossed to GOLDEN GARNETTE and one result was HONEY BUN, a Sweetheart with good production and very fragrant but lacking in depth of yellow color and stylish form. It resembled its pollen parent more in both respects. Arnie Ellis is shown as the sole inventor in Modern Roses 8 but the plant patent grant includes me. This reminds us of a few other similar mistakes in recording. Two AARS Winners recorded as the sole production of Ollie Weeks in Modern Roses 8 are co-inventions of him and me as recorded by the Patent Office. These are PERFUME DELIGHT and ARIZONA - both Hybrid Teas. (By agreement I had no financial interest in either these two or GYPSY, an AARS Winner for the Introduction Year 1973.) The Patent Office has certain guidelines that qualify invention. These include: (1) the making of a cross or the ordering or directing that the cross be made, and (2) the propagation of or the ordering or directing that a selection be propagated. As these two activities were a joint effort inevitably several generations of introductions require a statement of co-invention after the retirement of one of the co-inventors, (From five to ten years normally elapse after pollination to the actual marketing of a rose). This sort of circumstance arose in the carry-overs from Dr. Lammerts to me, from the carry-overs from me to Dr. David Armstrong, from me to

Ollie Weeks, from Dr. Armstrong to me, and from me to Jack Christensen. All were registered with The American Rose Society with the same credits that applied to invention except for PERFUME DELIGHT, ARIZONA, and HONEY BUN where only one of the co-inventors were named in Modern Roses. I am not faulting the editors of Modern Roses.

Chapter 16

NEW ZEALAND

The second World Rose Conference took place in New Zealand. I had been invited to be a part of the program but had a mild heart attack about a month before we were to leave (Helen, my wife, was to have gone with me) so the trip was canceled on doctor's advice. We decided to go the following year, however, and timed our trip to coincide with the Annual Convention of The National Rose Society of New Zealand at Wellington on the southern tip of North Island. I was invited to speak and to take part in judging a rose show held in connection with the Convention. Having toured both North and South Island prior to the Convention it was no surprise to find the show specimens of magnificent quality. The size of some of my own varieties made them strangers to me without labels. Our New Zealand experience included a visit to The Rhododendron Trust at the foot of Mount Egmont, called Mount Taranaki locally. This trust boasts supporting members from all over the world. Our timing was perfect as the rhododendrons were in full bloom and the collection included the world's finest varieties. The late Mr. and Mrs. Douglas Butcher (Doug and Esme) of Stratford were our guides on that tour. The Butchers then drove us to New Plymouth where we visited the world famed Duncan & Davies Ltd. (nursery). This was a great experience as I had imported many plants over the years from the collection of this firm on behalf of Armstrong Nurseries. It was not long after our visit that Victor Davies, then in his nineties, was knighted by Queen Elizabeth II of England. We were privileged to have dinner with him and Mrs. Victor Davies at the home of their son and daughter-in-law, Trevor and Mary Davies, where we were overnight guests.

Another pleasant experience was our visit to the rose park at Palmerston North, where we found a huge collection of roses in marvelous condition.   It is at the edge of Massey University where part of the curriculum concerns the training of agricultural and horticultural students.   The New Zealand tour was taken in October and November, the Spring of the year in the Southern Hemisphere.   We were enormously impressed with the beauty and uniqueness of this island country.

Chapter 17

CHANGING TIMES

By February 1973 substantial changes in management at Armstrong Nurseries made complete and final retirement seem timely for me. Arnold Ellis resigned together with all the top management including John A. Armstrong, Jr, then President of the Company. This left Jack Christensen in charge at the Research Department. He "inherited" all the seedlings, seed and crosses made by his predecessors. We (Arnie and I) had made selections that were already in the AARS Trials as well as some that were in production as cut-flower kinds for the florist trade. Armstrong Nursries had only one rose that was given an AARS Award for the Introduction year 1977. It was DOUBLE DE-LIGHT that resulted when GRANADA was crossed to GARDEN PARTY. The two parent varieties had similar color patterns but GRANADA, the smaller flowered one, had much the more intense coloring as well as marvelous fragrance. GARDEN PARTY had little fragrance, as might have been expected from its two only slightly fragrant parents. Truly, I wanted just what I got as to color, size of flower and form. I knew my chances were slim but I hoped, nevertheless, as all rose breeders must. I wished I might obtain a seedling with GRANADA'S color intensity. I got one somewhat brighter, a large flower approaching GARDEN PARTY in size, the trait of starting a red bud with an ivory center that changed to red as it opened - if the sun were shining. Experience had long before taught me that seldom did one get exactly what one desired in a cross. In this instance I not only got all I desired but some bonus qualities as well.   Bonus characters were the intensity of fragrance, the profusion of bloom and the trait of being one of the first roses in bloom in the spring - repeating often.   I think whoever named it chose a good name in suggesting pleasure for both the eyes and nose.   I was very pleased and gratified to learn that DOUBLE DELIGHT was voted "The Most Popular Rose In The World" at the last International Rose Conference in Canada.   I am pleased as punch to learn as this is written that it has been voted the "James Alexander Gamble Award for Fragrance" by The American Rose Society.

In the same AARS Trials were two other seedlings that did not receive awards but were introduced.   One was MARMALADE, obtained from ARLENE FRANCIS X BEWITCHED.   Dr. Lam- merts had obtained his 1967 AARS Award winner, BEWITCHED, by crossing QUEEN ELIZABETH X TAWNY GOLD.   It was a soft pink, suggesting a strong influence from TAWNY GOLD, described as "tawny gold" (which I deduced was a deep yellow).   I assumed from its parentage as well as from its appearance that it could be expected to transmit factors for yellow petal color.   It had excellent form in the flower with just the right number of petals.   A flaw was a frequent crook in a long peduncle.   ARLENE FRANCIS, a seedling of Gene Boerner's, was a bit shy of petals but had about the richest yellow flower among Hybrid Tea roses.   My aim was to select from the seedlings of this cross a vigorous plant with the rich yellow flowers of ARLENE FRANCIS, the petalage and form of BEWITCHED, the straight peduncle of ARLENE FRANCIS - and anything else "good" I could conceivably get from a composite of the two parents!   My best selection appeared to have everything our heart could desire except the flowers were only yellow on the outer surface of the petals and had only thirty petals at most.   The inner surfaces were coppery-orange and I hoped for a "reincarnation" of ORANGE NASSAU in this extremely vigorous and glossy leaved seedling.   The flower of ORANGE NASSAU had so enchanted me three decades earlier it had been my ambition to secure it on a good plant (which ORANGE NASSAU certainly did not have).   I still regard MARMALADE with affection but while it had a magnificent plant with huge glossy leaves suffice it to say - it's flower is not equal to that of ORANGE NASSAU and it did not get an AARS Award. As remembered it came in fourth behind DOUBLE DELIGHT in scoring.   Of some genetic interest was the selection of a sister seedling of DOUBLE DELIGHT that resembled GARDEN PARTY in both flower color and plant much more than its sister, and of course much less like GRANADA. It acquired the name SHIRLEY LAUGHARN when it was sold to a man for private distribution. I used it as a seed parent and pollinated it with an unnamed seedling from the cross of BEWITCHED X KING'S RANSOM. One of the resulting seedlings was named CANDLELIGHT, described as a "rich yellow with a pink tinge in the bud in the spring". Jack Christensen and I share credits on this one as he made the selection of it as a seedling.

Chapter 18

A GENETIC GUESS

Professor Gustav Mehlquist, University of Connecticutt, whom I had known when he was still at U.C.L.A., was famous for his research on the inheritance of color in delphiniums. As remembered he found the pigment essential to blue was most fully expressed when in association with a factor for ivory color. Out of curiosity I cast about for a rose variety with an ivory color to which I might cross ANGEL FACE. A seedling produced by David Armstrong and named MISTY seemed my best prospect as its parents MOUNT SHASTA and MATTERHORN were ivory colored offspring of QUEEN ELIZABETH, in turn the offspring of FLORADORA. MISTY, a Hybrid Tea, described as creamy white in color seemed more "ivory" to me. The decision to cross ANGEL FACE X MISTY did not lead me closer to blue. It did not even result in any lavender flowered seedlings as remembered. It did give me a seedling with flowers about as pure white as seen in roses. It was a Grandiflora in habit with flowers somewhat larger than ANGEL FACE, with that variety's fragrance and flower form. Jack Christensen selected it and multiplied it for AARS Entry. When it came through the Trials successfully with an AARS Award for the Introduction Year 1981 Jack proposed the name WHITE LIGHTNIN' and that name was approved and registered.

Apricot colored rose flowers have been characterized by color instability. The best varieties introduced before 1982 were APRICOT NECTAR, a Floribunda by Gene Boerner and

MEDALLION, a Hybrid Tea by William Warriner. Both were improvements on varieties previously available but neither were very color stable. A greenhouse cut-flower Hyrbid Tea variety named DR. A. J. VERHAGE, with the commercial synonym of GOLDEN WAVE, bred by G. Verbeek of Holland, had color superior to either of these but had such poor growth that it had very little distribution out-of-doors. I was emboldened to use it as a pollen parent in a cross with FIRST PRIZE in the hope that the independent places of origin might result in some hybrid vigor. Relying on the published parentage of FIRST PRIZE it seemed probable that it would contain genetic factors for yellow flowers. Another attraction in this cross was the very broad petals of FIRST PRIZE and to a lesser extent those of GOLDEN WAVE. Again Jack Christensen selected a Hybrid Tea offspring with good vigor and with the broad petal heritage from its parents. Its flower color was in the apricot range and while it was not as stable as I might have desired it was a definite improvement in that respect in its class. It won an AARS Award for the Introduction Year of 1982 and became the last variety with which I was associated to do so. Someone was inspired to name it BRANDY.

A few other seedlings started by me and carried forward to introduction by Jack Christensen through Armstrong Nurseries (now Armstrong Roses) were of lesser importance for either the cut-flower trade or garden use. Two of these deserve mention, though. SOUTHERN BELLE the product of a cross of PINK PARFAIT X PHOENIX, of which Arnie Ellis and I are co-inventors, was introduced in 1983. To the best of my knowledge it was the only seedling introduced from PHOENIX - and it was not for lack of trying. PHOENIX would not set seed and produced very little pollen. What pollen it did produce was not very viable. This was very frustrating as the variety had a remarkable collection of highly desirable qualities. These included excellent vigor, large glossy foliage with good mildew resistance, large flowers with broad petals and beautiful form from bud to full blown flower. The shade of red was cerise and that, with the lack of petal substance, were the principal shortcomings in an otherwise nearly perfect rose - except for its sterility!

KATHERINE LOKER from ZORINA X GOLDEN WAVE is a very nice Floribunda with large yellow flowers but won no awards of which I am aware. Its importance, as I see it, is its role as one of the parents of Jack Christensen's GOLD MEDAL, one of today's finest yellow roses in my opinion.

Chapter 19

REFLECTIONS

Roy Shepherd in his book, History of The Rose (1954), observed that LA FRANCE (Guillot - 1867) was widely recognized as representing a new class of rose and became known as the first Hybrid Tea. He noted that while it was seen as combining the delicacy of flower and everblooming qualities of the Tea Rose and the sturdy growth of Hybrid Perpetuals its parentage was a matter of speculation as controlled crossings were not practiced at that time. Therefore, the recorded parentage is what might be called an "educated guess". Guillot himself was somewhat dubious as to the parentage but other skilled rosarians of the day were confident it exhibited characters from MME. BRAVY (Tea) and MME. VICTOR VERDIER (Hybrid Perpetual) strongly enough to attach this probable parentage to LA FRANCE.

Shepherd also noted that LA FRANCE was not as important a parent as its phenotypic characters would seem to justify. It is noted that Modern Roses 6 gives it a chromosome count of 21 which would make it pretty much of a "mule" - a strongly sterile triploid. One cross, with LADY MARY FITZWILLIAM, was successful in producing MRS. W. J. GRANT in 1895, a more productive parent. By that time other Hybrid Tea varieties were coming along, some already on the market. Even so this was just a cueing up for the explosion of new Hybrid Teas to come in the Twentieth Century. French, English, Irish and German breeder-nurserymen were involved in the rush to produce new Hybrid Teas.

Jean-Baptiste Guillot of Lyon, France raised the first recognized Hybrid Tea but did not hold his lead. Henry Bennett of Shepperton, England raised LADY MARY FITZWILLIAM in 1882, apparently a more fertile parent than LA FRANCE. Joseph Perner-Ducher of France produced MME. CAROLINE TESTOUT in 1890 but his SOLEIL D'OR in 1900 really set the rose world a-buzz with its factor for bright yellow flower color from the wild rose, ROSA FOETIDA PERSIANA. Alexander Dickson of Northern Ireland introduced LIBERTY, a red descended from MRS. W. J. GRANT. Its descendants are legion from breeders all over the world.

Sam McGredy IV observed recently that this century has produced rose breeders who have advanced the quality of rose varieties for the world's gardens and florist shops to rival the advance in industrial technology. This seems a shrewd observation to me. Leaders in certain areas of rose breeding emerged. Pernet-Ducher stands out in my mind as "first among equals" because he gave us the base for such a quantity of new colors with his use of ROSA FOETIDA PERSIANA. He dominated the market for the first twenty five years with such roses as SOLEIL D'OR (1900), foundation of the so-called Pernetiana Class and the genuine deep yellow roses; CHATEAU DE CLOS VOGET (1908), fragrant deep red; JULIEN POTIN (1927), deep yellow with good bud form; MME. CAROLINE TESTOUT (1890) fragrant soft carmine pink, for many years the most prominent rose in Portland, Oregon; MME. EDOUARD HERRIOT (1913), fragrant coral-red and yellow, NRS Gold Medal; SOUV. DE CLAUDIUS PERNET (1920), sunflower yellow, Batatelle Gold Medal; VILLE DE PARIS (1925), bright yellow, Bagatelle Gold Medal and many others. Pernet-Ducher's curiosity and imagination took him a long way in the then still new Hybrid Tea roses.

Samuel McGredy II, Portadown, Northern Ireland came on strongly in the middle of Pernet-Ducher's activity no doubt using the latter's achievements as a spring-board to win Gold Medal after Gold Medal of the Royal National Rose Society of England for his novel new Hybrid Tea roses. Those that particularly impressed me with their novelty and merit were; MRS. HERBERT STEVENS (1910), white Hybrid Tea, RNRS Gold Medal; OLD GOLD (1913), with deep gold colored flowers was the first rose with buds I remember seeing with points at the apex of the petals flaring outward at the tips. This rose also won the RNRS Gold Medal and its bud form became my ideal; GOLDEN EMBLEM (1917),

RNRS Gold Medal, rich canary yellow with red blush on the bud -the richest color of yellow I had seen at the time it was first observed about 1929. THE QUEEN ALEXANDRA ROSE - according to Sam McGredy IV in his book, "A Family of Roses," is one of the parents of both MARGARET MCGREDY and MRS. SAM MCGREDY and through the former a forebear of PEACE. It was the parent of the spectacular striped sport, FIESTA. THE QUEEN ALEXANDRA ROSE was the first I had seen with bright red inner surfaces and bright yellow reverse. It won another RNRS Gold Medal. MARGARET MCGREDY IN 1927 and MRS. SAM MCGREDY IN 1929 both won the Gold Medal of the RNRS and established such a reputation for the firm of Samuel McGredy & Son that Samuel McGredy II found it astute merchandising to attach the McGredy name to a whole series of subsequent introductions, viz., MCGREDY'S YELLOW, MC-GREDY'S PEACH, MCGREDY'S IVORY etc. PICTURE (1932) did not win any awards that I know but while it had a somewhat small flower for a Hybrid Tea it was otherwise a near ideal. It is still in commerce after over fifty years and that is unusual indeed.

MRS. SAM MCGREDY was named in honor of the mother of Sam McGredy IV. He recognizes it as perhaps their most famous rose but he considers it an "indifferent breeder". I did not find this so as it was the mother of TAFFETA and the grandmother of FANDANGO which was in turn the mother of MONTEZUMA. MONTEZUMA was the parent of many important roses for me.

Svend Poulsen, of the firm of D. T. Poulsen Planteskole, Kvistgaard, Denmark felt the need of rose varieties that could withstand the colder winters of Scandinavia. Being aware of the greater cold hardiness of some of the varieties in the Polyantha Class and believing that increased flowers size would increase their attraction he made a cross of ORLEANS ROSE, Polyantha, with RED STAR, Hybrid Tea. One result was a seedling with semi-double two-toned pink flowers produced in large clusters. The individual flowers were much larger than those of ORLEANS ROSE and although not quite as cold hardy as that variety it was much more cold resistant than RED STAR, the Hybrid Tea parent. Poulsen named his new variety ELSE POULSEN after a member of his family. It was decided that it would be marketed under a new Class name, "Hybrid Polyantha". ELSE POULSEN was introduced about 1924 and other Hybrid Polyanthas from

Poulsen followed. It is believed the Poulsen hybrids were distributed in Europe with the class designation given them by Poulsen up to the time of World War II when rose distribution stopped throughout Europe.

Wilhelm Kordes of Sparrieshoop, Germany, a contemporary of Svend Poulsen was no doubt aware of Poulsen's activity. Whether he was influenced by it or not is not known. However, by the early 1930's he was involved in a project aimed at a somewhat similar objective. Kordes was introducing traits from the Musk Rose, ROSA MOSCHATA. By 1933 he had introduced EVA from a cross of ROBIN HOOD X J. C. THORNTON. ROBIN HOOD is classed as a Hybrid Musk and J. C. THORNTON is a Hybrid Tea. The flowers of ROBIN HOOD are similar in size to many varieties of the Polyantha Class and are borne in large clusters. As a result EVA resembled in flowering habit types from crosses being made by Poulsen. At any rate Kordes called EVA a Hybrid Musk which, of course, it was. A few years later he had a distribution agreement with Jackson & Perkins Company of Newark, New York. "J & P" had acquired a rose breeder, Dr. J. H. Nicolas, who in 1934 produced a rose bred from the Polyantha, ECHO and a Hybrid Tea, REV. F. PAGE-ROBERTS. They named it ROCHESTER and classed it a "Floribunda" - a newly coined Class name. From that time all Hybrid Musk originations from Kordes introduced by Jackson & Perkins became Floribundas in their catalogue. Gene Boerner, J & P's breeder after Dr. Nicolas' death, began making more advanced crosses of this nature. Many fine Floribunda varieties resulted from his work and they won many AARS Awards.

Dicksons of Hawlmark, Newtownards, Northern Ireland bred and introduced many fine Hybrid Tea and Floribunda varieties. Patrick Dickson, the current breeder and a contemporary of Sam McGredy IV, Reimer Kordes (son of Wilhelm), Niels Poulsen, Jack Harkness of Hitchin, Hertfordshire, England and Mathias Tantau II of Uetersen, Holstein, West Germany (breeder of TROPICANA) are all now in a diversified rose breeding program and are producing all types of new roses at a furious pace. Sam McGredy IV no longer does his breeding in Northern Ireland as he now lives and works in Auckland, New Zealand. He places just as much emphasis on disease resistance as he did in Northern Ireland. His OLYMPIAD in 1984 is in my opinion a giant step forward in red Hybrid Teas.

Dr. Walter E. Lammerts and I began the breeding line that resulted in the Grandiflora Class. His QUEEN ELIZABETH and my BUCCANEER and ROUNDELAY led the way. These all came on the market in the space of two or three years. My earliest emphasis was on vigor of plant and flower form. Dr. Lammerts was more successful in his search for disease resistance. Both of us, however, had as our primary objective a longer lasting flower. The additional vigor we obtained was not an altogether unexpected bonus to either of us. Each of us perhaps saw the unexpected results in a little different light. Neither of us pursued the breeding of Miniatures beyond an initial cross. I had an early impression that this trait was a recessive one but this now appears to have been incorrect.

Ralph S. Moore, Sequoia Nursery, Visalia, California was preceded by John deVink of Boskoop, Holland and Pedro Dot and San Feliu de Llobregat, Barcelona, Spain but not by very much. Ralph, by the middle 1930's, was intensely involved in producing new Miniature varieties and is still going strong. He has been very much the leader in popularizing this class in the United States -perhaps in the world. Ralph was recently awarded the Dean Hole Medal for his contribution and leadership in the growing of this class of rose. This has now become such a popular breeding subject that I fear it is in danger of being overdone. I can no longer keep track of the new varieties. One wonders how anyone can.

All successful rose breedrs, both amateur and professional are aware of the importance of novelty. There is no point to offering the public a new rose that is indistinguishable from one already on the market. It is encouraging indeed to see the improvement being made in all the classes of roses with respect to health. The numbers of American commercial breeders has shrunk and they are largely concentrated in Southern California as far as those concerned primarily with garden roses. The major exception is Ralph Moore in Central California.

Southern California, until the last few years, had experiencd little Blackspot. Powdery Mildew and Rose Rust, particularly the former, have been an affliction for years. When I first began breeding roses only Powdery Mildew was conspicuous enough to create concern in my mind. This was probably true for Dr. Lammerts too as he was introduced to roses at Armstrong Nurseries. While Powdery Mildew resistance was an objective of both Dr. Lammerts and me I think he was more consistent than me in his efforts to achieve his goals in this direction. I was not oblivious of the need as I discarded many seedlings for mildew susceptibility before ever seeing a flower on them.

All rose breeders have improved their strains for disease resistance over the course of their careers. None I think more so than Sam McGredy IV with respect to Powdery Mildew and Blackspot. Nature has helped him by providing a climate in both Northern Ireland and New Zealand where these organisms can flourish. More than this I want to give Sam credit for his production of many AARS Award Winners with these characters. He has managed to incorporate novelty of flower color, beautiful foliage, vigor and health of plant that any rose breeder should be glad to emulate.

Chapter 20

TWENTIETH CENTURY LEADERS

The following list of commercial rose breeders is a chronological one for the Twentieth Century thus far. In it I have attempted to point out the most important or significant direction of the breeder's work as I see it. In some instances this is exemplified by a particular variety so such varieties have been mentioned. I make no attempt to judge the relative importance except in the case of Joseph Pernet-Ducher whose contributions seems to me the most significant. Another French breeder might very well have overtaken him had it not been for his untimely death. This is Francis Meilland, the breeder of PEACE, BACCARA and CHARLES MALLERIN. The list is not complete and omits some who made important contributions to our gardens. It is not my intent to omit such but if names are omitted it is because they did not rise to the surface of my mind or perhaps have not yet had a long enough career to evaluate the characteristics of their output. The list follows:

1900 to 1925 — *Joseph Pernet-Ducher* — Innovative — incorporated genes from ROSA FOETIDA PERSIANA and probably R. FOETIDA BICOLOR into garden roses. SOLEIL D'OR was the starter.

1915 to 1930 — *Samuel McGredy II* — Imaginative — followed Pernet-Ducher and expanded. His most outstanding rose: MRS. SAM MCGREDY.

1925 to 1965 — *Wilhelm Kordes* — Innovative and imaginative

— used many species experimentally especially ROSA MOSCHATA - CRIMSON GLORY a most outstanding Hybrid Tea parent - BABY CHATEAU and PINOCCHIO (ROSENMARCHEN) in Floribunda equally important.

1925 to 1950 — *Mathias Tantau Sr.* — An aggressive experimenter he used Kordes' BABY CHATEAU to produce FLORADORA which with GARNETTE were very important to both garden and greenhouse rose production in both Europe and the United States.

1930 -- — *Dicksons of Hawlmark* — Secrecy was a family policy with respect to rose breeding until Pat Dickson, the current breeder. One consequence - many prize winning varieties but none impressed me as historically significant breeding material. Pat Dickson has changed this policy and his output holds its own with his contemporaries world wide. His REDGOLD, Floribunda and PRECIOUS PLATINUM, Hybrid Tea impress me the most.

1930 to -- — *Ralph S. Moore* — started in the late 1920's breeding Rambler and open pollinated Hybrid Tea seedlings but by 1940 he had begun to breed Miniature varieties and soon thereafter was introducing new varieties in that class regularly and still is as this is written. He has dominated this area of breeding activity for many years and now has a world wide amateur following.

1940 to 1970 — *Eugene S. Boerner* — Dominant world wide in production of prize winning Floribunda varieties - FIRST PRIZE, Hybrid Tea, a breakthrough in combination of bud form, petal width and flower size; in Floribundas led the world in important varieties - MASQUERADE, FASHION, SPARTAN and ZORINA among many. His Floribunda varieties dominated the cut flower market in the United States during his lifetime.

1940 to -- — *Dr. Walter E. Lammerts* — Scientific methods produced CHARLOTTE ARMSTRONG, CHRYSLER IMPERIAL and QUEEN ELIZABETH as very important parent varieties used by many breeders all over the world. His career a consistent search for resistance to Powdery Mildew.

1945 to 1980 — *Herbert C. Swim* — Concerned chiefly in production of award winning varieties - any combination of character traits composed of flower novelty in shape and/or color, plant vigor, disease resistance, foliage attractiveness, flower fragrance, etc. that might give a variety a competitive edge. Best varieties: SUTTER'S GOLD, CIRCUS, MISTER LINCOLN, ANGEL FACE, DOUBLE DELIGHT and BRANDY - all winning an AARS Award and some international awards.

1950 to 1987 — *William A. Warriner* - officially "Bill" did not become a rose breeder until about 1963. I give him credit for starting about 1950 - shortly after he came to work at Howard & Smith. Fred Howard's health was failing by that time and it was plain to see that Bill was the one there who had the best grasp of the relative value of the new varieties. His goals seem to have been similar to my own but with possibly more emphasis on varieties suited to the greenhouse cut-flower trade. (We do not have available a systematized list as Modern Roses editions published after the bulk of his work do not give the names of breeder's and their varieties under the breeder's name). His career was spent mostly at Jackson & Perkins Co.

1960 to -- — Many young breeders around the world including *Pat Dickson* of Northern Ireland, *Jack Harkness* of England, *Reimer Kordes* of Germany, *Niels Poulsen* of Denmark, *Alain Meilland and his mother, Luisette Meilland* of France, *Sam McGredy IV* of New Zealand have all made impressive contributions and all are still very active except Niels Poulsen and Reimer Kordes. The latter two have been succeeded by younger members of their families. *Jack Christensen* of California has begun an independent venture as a rose breeder and I have no doubt he will continue as he has in the past with many fine varieties in any Class he chooses to work in. *Seizo Suzuki* of Japan has shown his ability by capturing AARS Awards in the United States. I believe he has been a stimulus to rose breeding in Japan. Many Japanese breeders have been registering new rose names since Seizo started.

Chapter 21

WHAT'S OUT THERE

Looking back on a career spanning almost forty four years spent mostly with roses it seems that I experienced not just the fulfillment of a dream but of dream after dream. Along the way there were a lot of dreams, of course, that bore no fruit. Those that did were so very dominant in my emotions that failures were blotted out. In the beginning discouragement was often experienced as progress toward any meaningful activity seemed so slow that it often appeared to me that a creative role was not going to come my way. In retrospect though it would appear that my progress toward a rose breeding career could hardly have been more direct. Fortunately I was able to make a living doing something that was more like play than work. The passage of the Plant Patent Amendment to the Patent Act in 1930 laid the groundwork for commercial plant breeding. Many leaders of nursery companies, including Armstrong Nurseries, saw the opportunity and took advantage of it. Already involved in roses when Dr. Lammerts was employed to set up a Research Division directed toward plant breeding, I was blessed with an opportunity to be of use. One might say "I was in the right spot at the right time." Looking back it appears as though I was guided quite directly to a vocation that led to as much fulfillment as I can imagine.

All America Rose Selections has been a blessing to the rose industry - to nurseries and to rose gardeners alike. Mistakes have been made and sometimes individuals of The American Rose Society have been quick to take exception. Today AARS seems

133

generally accepted in spite of past mistakes as its positive role seems to be better understood with the perspective of time. Competition through AARS is open to anyone. Since the ultimate purpose of the organization is to focus on increased distribution of the roses selected for Awards the entry in the competition is best done through a rose nursery. They are in a position to grow the necessary plants for entry. If an Award is secured obviously a nursery must be involved to produce the plants for distribution on introduction and is in a better position to also distribute them. As this is written several amateur rose breeders have won AARS Awards and have introduced such through a selected AARS Member. A nursery is in the best position to assume the burden of industry-wide licensing. This involves the responsibility of advertising, licensing other responsible rose growers, collecting royalties as well as growing and selling plants from its own production. It usually involves the job of prosecuting a plant patent application through a plant patent attorney and most amateur rose breeders have little knowledge of how to go about that. Most introducing rose nurseries are eager to have an AARS Award Winner to sell and license. If they think you have a good rose any one of several of the members of AARS will be glad to put it through the Trials. If it wins an Award they will also be happy to handle it for you. You will need to allow them their rightful share of the royalty collected as the expenses will be considerable. If you have a good seedling you are in a position to negotiate the terms under which it will be introduced.

Every person who wants to be a rose breeder should belong to The American Rose Society and be as active in it as circumstances permit. The dues are modest and the information contained in the monthly magazine and Rose Annual provide both contact with other rose lovers and information. If there is an affiliated rose club near enough to you that attendance at regular meetings is practical you should become an active member of it, entering into all its activities except being a principal officer. If you are not already a qualified judge, certified by The American Rose Society, I think you will find that will add much to your feel of what others like in roses. Of course, no one with ambition to become a rose breeder is without ideas of what he (or she) would like to see in a rose. If you hope to see one of your creations on the market remember that it must be pleasing to others as well as to yourself. Association with rose fanciers will expand not only your knowledge but your information. It was my good fortune to work for and with Mr. J. Awdry Armstrong who was not only a nurseryman but an artist as well. His canvas was the rose garden. He had formed his own standards for the rose but became qualified as an Official Judge of The American Rose Society and acted as a judge in rose shows when asked and he could find the time. With Awdry lines in bud and flower were greatly to be admired. He liked long, slender buds with flaring tips so that in silhouette the right side had the shape of a slenderized "S". An early favorite was a rose from Walter Easlea of Essex, England, called LULU. It did indeed have beautiful bud form and no doubt Awdry's liking for it influenced Dr. Lammerts in using it in early crosses. This rose was an early model for bud form for me too but Dr. Lammerts' experience in using it did not encourage me to try for this form through the use of LULU. On the other hand the yellow, SOEUR (SISTER) THERESE, used in the making of CHARLOTTE ARMSTRONG passed to that offspring the precise same bud shape and that became everyone's ideal at Armstrong Nurseries, not only the bud form but the flower form as well. As the flower opens it retains a high center and more than a hint of the bud form may be seen until the flower has completely unfolded. At least one breeder remarked that he "could spot Swim's roses by their trade-mark" -meaning, I think, that Awdry's influence was permanently implanted as far as bud shape was concerned. Moreover, as acquaintance with rose lovers endured it became apparent that these standards prevailed widely. In judging rose shows these qualities were to be seen most prominently in the "Queen of Show."

I do not want to leave the impression that the only rewards in rose breeding are monetary or based on successful competition. On the contrary the feeling of involvement in this creative act and seeing the phenomenon you have set in motion are truly fulfilling and you will feel rewarded by the privilege of witnessing the marvelous thing you have helped to bring about. You will discover that you experience some pride in your product whether it is a "world-beater" or not and I think that is as it should be. The Irish rosarian-writer, Sean McCann, a frequent contributor of entertaining articles for The American Rose Magazine, wrote several months ago a charming tale of his own experience as a rose breeder. If the hobby interests you give it a try. You will be in for some fun.

Chapter 22

— ADDENDUM —

Useful words from Dr. Walter E. Lammerts

Dr. Walter E. Lammerts was my mentor and the breeder of many famous roses, among them CHARLOTTE ARM-STRONG, CHRYSLER IMPERIAL and QUEEN ELIZABETH. He wrote some instructions for amateur rose breeders which he passed on to me. I think they are practical and could be very useful so have asked his permission to include them here.

He writes:

"Most people, when they ask you how to hybridize roses, actually mean how do you cross pollinate them. Fortunately professional hybridizers long ago found out that it is not necessary to place paper or other kinds of bags over the flowers which are to be used as pollen and seed parents. When the sepals, petals and anthers are removed, bees, bee flies and other insects which cross pollinate roses and other flowers are no longer interested. What is left are the pistils at the bottom of which are the ovules that will become the future seeds when they are fertilized (pollinated) by the nucleus in the germinating pollen tube. The anthers which contain the pollen may be gathered when the flower is in the late bud stage. When placed on sheets of paper and put in the sun they soon split open, allowing the pollen to be deposited on the paper. It may be poured into small glass jars and will remain viable

for several days if kept in a cool room when not in use. (Do not place in a refrigerator when in a container as they will sweat and mold.) When you wish to pollinate the flowers you have selected simply bend them over gently and rub the tops of the pistils (the stigma) in the pollen and the job is done. (If you haven't much pollen for the job you want to do you may find you can make your pollen go further by using an artist's small paint brush). Then label the pollinated flower as to what the cross was in terms of the variety used and it will soon develop into a gradually ripening hip (seed pod). If the pollinations are finished by late May or early June the hips will turn yellow, and even at times tinged with red, indicating that they are ripe and ready to harvest by late September or early October.

Now, though professional rose breeders plant the seeds from these ripened hips in 'flats' or other types of containers and then place them in cold storage for three months at 40 degrees F. it is not necessary for the amateur rose breeder to go to this expense. Simply place the seeds in moist (but not soaking wet) planting mix, of which various sorts are marketed - all very good as a rule. Then put this mixture of seeds and planting mix in ziploc bags using one for each group of cross-pollinated seeds. Place the collection of bags in a small carton in the 40 degrees F. part of your refrigerator for three months and when planted the viable seeds will quickly germinate. In fact some will start germinating right in the refrigerator! Should you live in the colder parts of the United States the placing of the seeds in the refrigerator will have to be delayed of course so that when the seeds germinate it will be warm enough to transplant them out of doors into containers such as the black plastic ones discarded by nurserymen after they have sold the plants grown in them. Many helpful hints as to techniques of cross polination, seed germination and selection of worthwhile seedlings may be obtained from the Newsletters of the Rose Hybridizers Association consisting of about six hundred members. Membership dues are minimal and the information is well worth the membership fee.

Now, when it comes to the subject of rose hybridization you are faced with a more complex problem than merely cross pollination. You can have fun making crosses and growing seedlings without knowledge of plant genetics but some knowledge of Mendelian behavior will be most helpful and enhance both your pleasure and your opportunities. A study of the parentage of roses you know (in the latest version of Modern Roses, distributed by The American Rose Society) will afford you many clues as to what has already been accomplished as well as how it was done. Much of the success of hybridization is due to intuitive knowledge gained either by experience or carefully reading just what successful rose breeders actually used in the way of rose varieties to accomplish their objectives. It is hoped that the reading of this book may prove helpful to those of you seriously interested in reaching certain objectives. One can often greatly profit by studying not only other people's successes but their failures as well."

Chapter 23

EXPERIMENTING

Rose breeding is an operation in exploring new ideas exercising one's curiosity - trying new avenues of obtaining goals greatly desired and not yet attained with a degree of success satisfying to the breeder. When I go into rose gardens or a nursery where roses are in bloom, I often find myself in a reverie these days wishing to see the seedlings that might result from various crosses. They are mostly fairly obvious so no doubt many or perhaps most of them have been tried. However, knowing that others had made "my crosses" would not deter me from making them unless I had seen the results from another's effort and found the "composite" of their resulting population totally discouraging. Here are some of the crosses I would make in sufficient quantity to get a cross-section of results and satisfy my curiosity:

BRANDY X NEW YEAR — An attempt to combine the broad petals and large flower size of BRANDY with richer flower color of NEW YEAR - near to the apricot color approached by BRANDY. Both parents should give great vigor and fine foliage to the population. Unfortunately both parent varieties have some of the same shortcomings - small prickles on the peduncle and long ones on the stems - large and broad on BRANDY and long and sharp on NEW YEAR. Both parents should assure good resistance to Powdery Mildew and attractive glossy leaves. Some unexpected colors could result. NEW YEAR has the quality of starting color near apricot and finishing near copper. I would take that in a flower with BRANDY's other characters!

BRANDY X GINGERSNAP — An attempt to get much the same result as in the previous cross. In this case the prickle problem should be under control. GINGERSNAP has almost smooth peduncles and the prickles elsewhere are of modest size. The copper-orange color of GINGERSNAP is truly novel. It would be sensational in a Hybrid Tea if this cross should produce it. The problem might be flower size.

BRANDY X SUTTER'S GOLD — The effort here is to get a seedling with the broad petals of BRANDY in any pleasant shade of yellow, the foliage of either parent, the reduced prickles of SUTTER'S GOLD, except on the peduncle where SUTTER'S GOLD has soft ones. The question here would be the color. If it were intermediate it perhaps would not be desirable.

BRANDY X MARMALADE — The objective here would be to get yellows in a range from sunflower yellow to copper. The vigor of the progeny and the size and gloss of the leaves should be generally good. Petalage might tend to be shy and prickles might tend to be large but there should not be too many of them. I would hope for few prickles on the peduncles as MARMALADE has few. The flowers could be huge as both parents can contribute this character.

BRANDY X MOJAVE — Hopefully similar results might be obtained from this as in the cross with SUTTER'S GOLD but perhaps with a better chance of copper-orange color in the flowers. Foliage size, texture, and quantity should be satis-factory. Possibly the quantity of petals might be a problem here.

BRANDY X REDGOLD — The aim here is similar to that in the cross to SUTTER'S GOLD but with better petal substance. There would probably be a tradeoff in that flower size would be somewhat smaller.

BRANDY X ORANGE PARFAIT — This is to be a curiosity satisfier. The color results should be in the general area in which I feel there is a need - apricot-orange. Quality flowers should be possible and the foliage and plants of the resulting seedlings should be generally good.

If I were doing these crosses I would try to do the reciprocal (the reverse) of all the crosses as well. It has been my experience that there is little, if any, difference in the seedlings but there is sometimes considerable difference in the way seed is set and often as much variation in the way the seed germinates.

ROUNDELAY X OKLAHOMA — A seedling from ROUNDE-LAY X CRIMSON GLORY produced WAR DANCE, a rose with truly novel color. The habit was awkward-spreading and the prickles were so thick, that it spoiled the variety as a cut flower. OKLAHOMA could have the color genes of CRIMSON GLORY and could give its offspring much better plant habit and larger flowers than CRIMSON GLORY. Worth a try.

ROUNDELAY X MISTER LINCOLN — Same objective as above. Would not try the reciprocal of this as seed of MISTER LINCOLN has been difficult to germinate.

ROUNDELAY X PHOENIX (if you can get it) — Exploratory for color inheritance. These two roses complement one another well. PHOENIX has large, glossy leaves, neat habit, broad petals and big flowers. Its petals are soft but ROUNDELAY's are not. This cross could result in very dark red flowers that burn, but it could give some very bright red flowers too.

MARMALADE X ORANGE PARFAIT — Would hope this might result in vigorous seedlings with MARMALADE colors but with somewhat better definition - lemon yellow outer surfaces with copper-orange inner surfaces. Would hope for the plant habit of MARMALADE to predominate. Likewise MARMALADE foliage.

MARMALADE X MISTER LINCOLN — Certainly should have vigorous seedlings from this cross. Would expect large, glossy leaves, very large flowers with some degree of fragrance. There should be some reds among the offspring but their exact shade is problematical. Would not attempt the reciprocal - too difficult to germinate.

OLYMPIAD X MARMALADE — Similar to preceding cross but somewhat smaller flowers and with generally better form.

GINGERSNAP X MARMALADE — Hope for intermediate

plant character and redistribution of flower color. Would assume the probability of flower size being intermediate. Would hope for GINGERSNAP inner flower surfaces and possibly outer flower surfaces of MARMALADE. Would need a fairly large population to fully explore this.

GOLD MEDAL X MARMALADE — A combination of two very vigorous yellow flowered parents, both with well formed buds and flowers and with variable influence of red and yellow and both with large, glossy foliage. The quite different shades and patterns of yellow in the parents should lead to interesting recombinations in the progeny.

GOLD MEDAL X BRANDY — Almost surely this has been tried but so far nothing has appeared on the market from it. We doubt that the possibilities have been thoroughly explored. Both parent varieties have fine vigor, glossy foliage, mildew resistance, fine bud form and broad petaled open blooms. GOLD MEDAL's relative freedom from prickles should satisfactorily reduce the size and quantity of prickles on BRANDY - not that BRANDY is seriously flawed in this respect, but it could be improved.

MARMALADE X MADRAS — This would be an attempt to get a flower of large size with the color of ORANGE NASSAU. ORANGE NASSAU had a coppery-orange inner petal color and bright yellow reverse. This combination of flower color has been a goal of mine ever since I first saw the magnificent flower on a miserable plant exhibited by this variety in the 1940's. Both parent prospects in this cross have petals with yellow reverse but neither have quite the copper orange that ORANGE NASSAU showed on it's inner surfaces but both approach it and are complementary in this respect.

Chapter 24

SWIM ROSES
IN CHRONOLOGICAL ORDER

(ARS Registry or Introduction Dates)

1945 — PRINCESS ANGELINE =
        Charlotte Armstrong X (Mrs. Sam McGredy X
        Pres. Herbert Hoover)

1947 — PINKIE =
        China Doll (open pollinated) ·················· AARS

1947 — NOCTURNE =
        Charlotte Armstrong X Night ··············· AARS

1948 — MULTNOMAH =
        Contrast X Charlotte Armstrong

1948 — ROSE OF FREEDOM =
        Charlotte Armstrong X Night

1949 — APPLAUSE =
        Contrast X Charlotte Armstrong ·······················*

1949 — FORTYNINER =
        Contrast X Charlotte Armstrong ············· AARS

1949 — TALLYHO =
        Charlotte Armstrong X Dickson's Red ······ AARS

1950 — FANDANGO =
   Charlotte Armstrong X (Mrs. Sam McGredy X Pres. Herbert Hoover)

1950 — JUNO =
   Duquesa de Penaranda X Charlotte Armstrong

1950 — PARAMOUNT =
   Charlotte Armstrong X Glowing Sunset

1950 — RED JACKET =
   World's Fair X Mirandy

1950 — SUTTER'S GOLD =
   Charlotte Armstrong X Signora--*--@--J--AARS

1951 — BRAVO =
   World's Fair X Mirandy

1951 — CHIEF SEATTLE =
   Charlotte Armstrong X Signora

1951 — FIRST LOVE =
   Charlotte Armstrong X Show Girl

1951 — HELEN TRAUBEL =
   Charlotte Armstrong X Glowing Sunset-&- AARS

1951 — VALENTINE =
   China Doll X World's Fair

1952 — ANGELIQUE =
   World's Fair X Pinocchio

1952 — ANNETTE =
   Charlotte Armstrong X Contrast

1952 — BEACON =
   Christopher Stone X Charlotte Armstrong

1952 — BIG DADDY =
   Crimson Glory X Texas Centennial

1952 — BUCCANEER =
Golden Rapture X (Max Krause X Captain Thomas) -- @

1953 — BAGDAD =
Charlotte Armstrong X Signora

1953 — EMBERS =
World's Fair X Floradora

1953 — FROLIC =
World's Fair X Pinocchio

1953 — GAY LADY =
Charlotte Armstrong X Piccaninny

1953 — LA JOLLA =
Charlotte Armstrong X Contrast

1953 — MIA MAID =
Charlotte Armstrong X Signora

1954 — LEMON CHIFFON =
Sister Therese X Golden Dawn

1954 — LOUISIANA PURCHASE =
Charlotte Armstrong X Piccaninny

1954 — MOJAVE =
Charlotte Armstrong X Signora ----*----@----AARS

1954 — MRS. LUTHER BURBANK =
Christopher Stone X Charlotte Armstrong

1954 — PINK FROST =
Charlotte Armstrong X Texas Centennial

1954 — REDCAP =
World'sFair X Pinocchio

1954 — ROUNDELAY =
Charlotte Armstrong X Floradora ------------------ @

147

1954 — SUGAR PLUM =
        Crimson Glory X Girona

1955 — GOLDSTRIKE =
        Goldilocks X Pinocchio

1955 — MONTEZUMA =
        Fandango X Floradora ·······························@·····%

1955 — WILDFIRE =
        World's Fair X Pinocchio

1956 — CIRCUS =
        Fandango X Pinocchio ·················@·····%····AARS

1956 — FANFARE =
        Fandango X Pinocchio ······························&

1956 — FORT VANCOUVER =
        Charlotte Armstrong X (Mrs. Sam McGredy
        X Pres. Herbert Hoover)

1956 — MIDNIGHT =
        Gay Lady X Texas Centennial

1956 — MOONSPRITE =
        Sutter's Gold X Ondine ·························&

1957 — AZTEC =
        Charlotte Armstrong X Unnamed Seedling

1957 — CATHAY =
        Fandango X Pinocchio

1957 — MANITOU =
        Charlotte Armstrong X Signora

1957 — STARLET =
        Goldilocks X (Fandango X Pinocchio)

1958 — GREEN FIRE =
        Goldilocks X (Fandango X Pinocchio)

1958 — HEAT WAVE =
    Unnamed Seedling X Roundelay

1958 — RED GLORY =
    Gay Lady X (Pinocchio X Floradora)

1958 — RUBY LIPS =
    World's Fair X Pinocchio

1958 — WAR DANCE =
    Roundelay X Crimson Glory - S & W

1958 — WHITE CHARM =
    Pinocchio X Virgo - S & W

1959 — CHERRY GLOW =
    Floradora X First Love

1959 — EL CAPITAN =
    Charlotte Armstrong X Floradora

1959 — GARDEN PARTY =
    Charlotte Armstrong X Peace ------------- * ---- AARS

1959 — HIGH TIME =
    Charlotte Armstrong X Signora

1959 — PINAFORE =
    China Doll X Mrs. Dudley Fulton

1960 — COUNTY FAIR =
    Frolic X Pink Bountiful

1960 — DUET =
    Fandango X Roundelay ---------------------------- AARS

1960 — MERRY HEART =
    El Capitan X Unnamed Seedling

1960 — PINK PARFAIT =
    First Love X Pinocchio ---------------------- % ---- AARS

149

1960 — JACK O'LANTERN =
      Circus X Golden Scepter - S & W

1961 — ALLURE =
      Mrs. Pierre S. du Pont X Charlotte Armstrong

1961 — FIRST LADY =
      First Love X Roundelay

1961 — INVITATION =
      Charlotte Armstrong X Signora - S & W

1962 — IMPERIAL GOLD =
      Charlotte Armstrong X Girona

1962 — JOHN S. ARMSTRONG =
      Charlotte Armstrong X Seedling ---------------AARS

1962 — SIX FLAGS =
      First Love X Roundelay

1962 — SUMMER SUNSHINE =
      Buccaneer X Lemon Chiffon

1962 — COLUMBUS QUEEN =
      La Jolla X Unnamed Seedling - with DLA

1962 — HAWAIIAN SUNSET =
      Charlotte Armstrong X Signora - S & W

1962 — MISTY PINK =
      Verona X Escort (not registered) - S & W

1962 — ROYAL HIGHNESS =
      Virgo X Peace - S & W ---------------$----F----AARS

1963 — EIFFEL TOWER =
      First Love X (C. Armstrong X Signora)
                           ----&----@----DLA

1963 — GRAND SLAM =
      Charlotte Armstrong X Montezuma - DLA

1963 — MATTERHORN =
Buccaneer X Cherry Glow-----with DLA-----AARS

1963 — ESCORT =
Spartan X Garnette - S & W

1963 — MOUNT SHASTA =
Queen Elizabeth X Blanche Mallerin - S & W

1963 — TOWN TALK =
(Circus X Garnette) X Spartan - S & W

1963 — VERONA =
Spartan X Garnette - S & W

1964 — BLITHE SPIRIT =
Fandango X Unnamed Seedling - DLA

1964 — JOSEPH'S COAT =
Buccaneer X Circus-------------with DLA-------------*

1964 — SWEET AFTON =
(Charlotte Armstrong X Signora) X (Alice Stern
X Ondine) - with DLA

1964 — CAMELOT =
Circus X Queen Elizabeth - S & W ----------AARS

1964 — LILAC DAWN =
Lavender Pinocchio X Frolic - S & W

1964 — MISTER LINCOLN =
Chrysler Imperial X Charles Mallerin -
S & W--------------------------AARS

1964 — OKLAHOMA =
C. Imperial X C. Mallerin - S & W

1964 — PLAIN TALK =
Spartan X Garnette - S & W

151

1964 — SWEET TALK =
Frolic X Lavender Pinocchio - S & W

1965 — FANCY TALK =
Spartan X Garnette - S & W

1965 — ORANGE GARNET =
(Garnette X Circus) X Spartan - S & W

1965 — WHITE SATIN =
Mount Shasta X White Butterfly - S & W

1966 — LUCKY LADY =
Charlotte Armstrong X Cherry Glow - DLA -
AARS

1966 — LEMON SPICE =
Helen Traubel X Unnamed Seedling - DLA

1966 — SEVENTH HEAVEN =
Seedling X Chrysler Imperial- DLA

1966 — GOLDEN SHEEN =
Ophelia X Circus - S & W

1966 — PINK FLAIR =
Verona X Escort - S & W

1968 — ANGEL FACE =
(Circus X Lavender Pinocchio) X Sterling Silver
S & W --+----AARS

1968 — COMANCHE =
Spartan X (Carrousel X Happiness) - S & W -
AARS

1968 — NIGHT 'N' DAY =
(World's Fair X Chrysler Imperial) X Happiness
S & W

1968 — PALOMA =
Mount Shasta X White Knight - S & W

1969 — BIENVENU =
Camelot X (Montezuma X War Dance) - S & W

1969 — SMALL TALK =
Yellow Pinocchio X Circus - S & W

1971 — SONRISA =
Mister Lincoln X Night 'N' Day - S & W

1971 — SUNRISE-SUNSET =
Tiffany X (Seedling X Happiness) - S & W

1972 — GYPSY =
[(Happiness X Chrysler Imperial) X El Capitan]
X Comanche - S & W--------------------------------AARS

1973 — HAPPY TALK =
Escort X Orange Garnet - S & W

1973 — PERFUME DELIGHT =
Peace X [(Happiness X Chrysler Imperial) X El
Capitan] - S & W--------------------------------AARS

1973 — HONEY BUN =
Goldstrike X Golden Garnette - AWE

1973 — ARIZONA =
[(Fred Howard X G. Scepter) X G. Rapture] X
[F. Howard X G. Scepter) X G. Rapture] - S & W
AARS

1975 — ANN FACTOR =
Duet X Jack O'Lantern - with AWE

1976 — RUBY RUFFLES =
(not registered) - with AWE

1977 — BARBIE =
Escort X Jazz Fest - with AWE

153

1977 — DOUBLE DELIGHT =
Granada X Garden Party - with AWE
-----@-----$-----J-----AARS

1977 — KRISTI =
White Satin X Bewitched - with AWE

1977 — MARMALADE =
Arlene Francis X Bewitched - " AWE

1980 — KATHERINE LOKER =
Zorina X Golden Wave- " JEC

1981 — WHITE LIGHTNIN' =
Angel Face X Misty - with JEC-----------------AARS

1982 — BRANDY =
First Prize X Golden Wave - " JEC-----------AARS

1982 — FIRST LADY NANCY =
American Heritage X First Prize - JEC

1982 — JENNIFER HART =
Pink Parfait X Yuletide - with JEC

1982 — ANITA =
Rumba X Marmalade - with JEC

1983 — SOUTHERN BELLE =
Pink Parfait X Phoenix - with AWE

1983 — CONFETTI =
Jack O'Lantern X Zorina - with JEC

1983 — CANDLELIGHT =
Shirley Laughran X (Bewitched X King's Ransom) with JEC

1983 — DANA =
White Satin X Bewitched - with JEC

```
AARS =    All-American Rose Selections Award
@     =    Geneva Gold Medal
*     =    Bagatelle Gold Medal
&     =    Rome Gold Medal
$     =    Madrid Gold Medal
%     =    Gold Medal Royal National Rose Society of
          England
```

The following are all awards of The American Rose Society:

```
+     =    John Cook Medal
F     =    David Fuerstenberg Prize
G     =    Gertrude M. Hubbard Gold Medal
J     =    James Alexander Gamble Medal for Fragrance
```

After 1958 many of my roses were the product of "co-invention" with others.   Such are indicated by the use of initials of the co-inventors.   The initials represent the men as follows:

```
S & W =    Swim & Weeks, a partnership between Herbert
           C. Swim and O.L. Weeks existing between 1955
           and 1967, inclusive.

DLA   =    Dr. David L. Armstrong

AWE   =    Arnold W. Ellis

JEC   =    Jack E. Christensen
```

In all instances I was the senior breeder.

INDEX